REACH YOUR GOALS
without stressing out

Chantal Hofstee is a clinical psychologist and executive coach, who specializes in stress management and leadership training. Chantal draws on her knowledge of the brain and psychology to explain the concepts of mindfulness-based thinking and teaches practical techniques that induce the ideal brain state for focus, productivity and performance. Her work is helping people to thrive in their everyday (work) life and has been called 'gently life-changing'; and 'transformational'. Her first book, *Mindfulness on the Run*, was published internationally by Exisle Publishing and was very well received. To find out more about Chantal and her work, visit www.drchantalhofstee.com

REACH YOUR GOALS
without stressing out

A high-achiever's guide
to a successful life

~

Chantal Hofstee

Clinical psychologist and executive coach

First published 2018

Exisle Publishing Pty Ltd
PO Box 864, Chatswood, NSW 2057, Australia
226 High Street, Dunedin, 9016, New Zealand
www.exislepublishing.com

A CiP record for this book is available from the National Library of Australia.

ISBN 978 1 925335 64 4

33614080709784

Designed by Enni Tuomisalo
Illustrations by Enni Tuomisalo
Typeset in PT Serif, 11pt
Printed in China

This book uses paper sourced under ISO 14001 guidelines from well-managed forests and other controlled sources.

10 9 8 7 6 5 4 3 2 1

Disclaimer

This book is a general guide only and should never be a substitute for the skill, knowledge and experience of a qualified medical professional dealing with the facts, circumstances and symptoms of a particular case. The nutritional, medical and health information presented in this book is based on the research, training and professional experience of the author, and is true and complete to the best of their knowledge. However, this book is intended only as an informative guide; it is not intended to replace or countermand the advice given by the reader's personal physician. Because each person and situation is unique, the author and the publisher urge the reader to check with a qualified healthcare professional before using any procedure where there is a question as to its appropriateness. The author, publisher and their distributors are not responsible for any adverse effects or consequences resulting from the use of the information in this book. It is the responsibility of the reader to consult a physician or other qualified healthcare professional regarding their personal care. The intent of the information provided is to be helpful; however, there is no guarantee of results associated with the information provided.

For Sem and Isha

99

PRAISE FOR CHANTAL'S FIRST BOOK,
MINDFULNESS ON THE RUN:

'Mindfulness on the Run *is rich in short techniques for keeping stress at a minimum, emotions in check, and relationships happy. A kind of psychologist in your head as you live life, that over time will fade to just being mindful.*'

— *Chelsea Houghton*

'*If you're one of the people who says you would be more mindful if only you had the time for it, this is your book. It can quickly become a friend in your search for greater peace, ease, and joy.*'

— *Krysta Gibson*, New Spirit Journal

'*Think you are too busy to practice mindfulness? This program is for you.*'

— Good Health Magazine

'I will definitely be recommending this well-written and researched practical handbook to others who are seeking a resource that is easy to read, informative and supports their busy lifestyles.'

— *Kirsty O'Callaghan, Unity Words*

'... simply don't have time for anything else? This book offers a quick and effective program to help slot mindfulness into your life.'

— Better Homes and Gardens

'As Dr Hofstee effectively demonstrates, not only do we need mindfulness most when we are busy, but when we have the right tools, it is possible to practise it on even the tightest schedule. This book is worth your time.'

— *Claire Nana*, Psych Central

~

CONTENTS

~

How to create sustainable, stress-free success

~

Edit your life frequently and ruthlessly.
It is your masterpiece after all.

— *Nathan W Morris*

~

Some days we are at our best. We have plenty of energy. We are focused and on track with what we want to accomplish that day, enjoying the process as much as the outcome and moving mountains of work without feeling drained or exhausted.

Then there are days when we have hardly any energy at all. We are busy, constantly distracted and wasting our energy on everything but the very things we really want to focus on. Our mind is blurred by brain fog and we feel sluggish and tired even though we get hardly anything done. Doing the little things feels like moving mountains, which can tip us over the edge and make us feel overwhelmed, frustrated or defeated.

Before I started to train my brain with mindfulness techniques, most of my days would fit description number two. It wasn't that I was unhappy with my life, but my body and my brain weren't functioning the way they should. This made everyday life so much harder and resulted in high levels of stress. I had clear goals of what I wanted to accomplish, but some days every step of the way felt like a battle. I clearly remember one of those days when simply posting a letter felt like running a marathon. I was on my way to burnout.

Now with a trained and healthy brain and a better work–life balance, I have a tight rein on my stress levels. This has made life so much better and easier. Stress no longer drains my energy and worries no longer occupy my mind. I reach my goals faster, I have more energy, I have better focus and most days feel easy and effortless.

Despite the changes I made being truly life-changing, I still found that some days I should have been more productive, more focused, more energized and more in control. There were still days when I felt tired and got stuck in habits that no longer worked for me. Even though the stressed out 'red brain' moments had been eliminated from my life for the most part, I couldn't help but wonder: could there be a next level to this? Were there more changes I could make to eliminate the blah days completely? Could I truly live from the 'green brain' every single day and reach my goals without stressing out?

As a result of my growing brain strength my life goals had started growing too. You could compare it to an athlete building up muscular strength and fitness; as your brain strength grows so do your goals. Not because you are unhappy with what you have and what you can do, but because of the inherent desire to grow, to learn and to master new skills. I found myself in a cycle of growing brain fitness and mental strength as a result of setting bigger goals, which in turn led me to needing even more brain and mental strength to accomplish them. So I wondered whether there was a new and better way for me to be more productive and to keep stress at bay even when striving for bigger things.

This question saw me embark on a journey of rethinking the areas of my life that are linked to productivity. Combining scientific research, psychology, mindful awareness and other methods I had been using to help clients create change, I rediscovered powerful 'brain hacks' that have helped me create a life structure that allows me to bring my best self to everything I do. This next phase of my 'life edit' has again been life-changing.

By examining different areas of life and applying both commonsense and scientific research to rethinking daily habits and routines, I have found a way of being productive that *gives* energy rather than burns it. It isn't that I wasn't being productive to begin with, but this time around my productivity is different and better than it was. I call it 'stress-free productivity'.

Stress-free productivity

My definition of stress-free productivity is:

~

Mindfully working towards your goals with focus, energy, passion and perseverance in a way that gives you lasting enjoyment of both the process and the outcome.

~

The stress-free productivity recipe includes the following ingredients:

1. a green brain
2. clear goals
3. focus
4. energy

5. passion

6. perseverance

7. enjoyment of the process, and

8. enjoyment of the outcome.

All these ingredients originate from knowledge about the brain. Knowing the ingredients, understanding how they work and then implementing them, gives a new approach to being productive. In the following chapters we will explore the different ingredients one by one and discover how you can mix them together to create your own recipe for reaching your goals by living mindfully with focus, passion and energy so you can keep going without burning out. The very first step to better, more sustainable productivity is to switch on the optimal brain state for productivity — the green brain.

INSIGHT QUESTIONS

Throughout this book you'll find pages titled 'Insight Questions'. I urge you to commit to answering these questions as you get to them, rather than skipping them or telling yourself that you'll do them 'later'. The Insight Questions are actually carefully prepared exercises that help turn the knowledge you gain into lasting change in your life.

The green brain

~

You have a superpower:
it is called the green brain.

~

As a psychologist, my area of expertise is the brain. The brain is an extremely complex organ and science has only been able to unravel a small part of how it works. You don't need to know all that science has discovered about the brain, but having a basic understanding of how your brain works can be helpful.

Not so long ago, most people's productivity consisted of physical labour — working on the land, working in a factory and doing manual housework. But today, our lives and goals have changed drastically and rely less on physical strength and more and more on mental resources and productivity. Yet the productivity models (and myths) and work systems we use and believe in are mostly rooted in the old productivity model that was based on achieving optimum productivity in physical labour. Those models, for the most part at least, don't apply to the brain and, as a result, we are seeing more and more people who burn out, are unhappy, and feel anxious and depressed. Stress has become a normal part of life even though it doesn't have to be. I believe that if we could only understand our biggest resource, the brain, we would approach productivity very differently.

It is rare to find an individual who knows even a little about how the brain works. This knowledge isn't taught in schools, it isn't part of the dialogue in the media and often parents are not teaching their children how the brain works because they themselves don't know. Yet more and more demands are being made on the brain and our mental resources, so a good place to start when it comes to rethinking your approach to productivity is to learn about the basics of the brain.

When it comes to the brain there are three 'settings': the red brain, the orange brain and the green brain.

The red brain

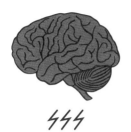

RED BRAIN

Instead of explaining the facts of what happens when you are in a red brain state, I suggest we do a little experiment so you can experience the red brain first-hand. Imagine a child running onto a road and there is a car coming at high speed. Close your eyes and imagine this, just for a moment. Watch this image of the child, the road and the car coming at the child at high speed.

Did you feel your heart beating faster, your breathing becoming shallow and the tension in your muscles tightening, especially around your neck and shoulders? Can you still feel the knot in your stomach? Was there pressure on your chest and the urge to act, to react and to reach out? This is stress. To be more precise, this is your system being flushed with the stress hormones adrenaline and cortisol to make you react effectively in emergency situations — the fight-or-flight response. This response is your body pumping blood faster to transport increased amounts of oxygen to your muscles to turn you into a faster runner and a better fighter.

In order to pull off this emergency response, which uses up so much of the body's available energy, all else needs to be put on hold. This means all natural bodily functions such as the need for sleep, your digestive system, your immune system, even your sex drive, are suppressed.

Now imagine that same scene of the child running onto the road and the car coming at high speed. However, this time, there is a person standing between you and the child. Just close your eyes for a moment and picture that scenario and pay attention to how you feel about this person and how you would react.

Did you feel the urge to push them aside, yell at them to get out of the way, without even considering their feelings? Notice that in that situation you are unable to put yourself in their shoes, and kindness, empathy and connection simply aren't available. Again, this is stress.

Stress gives you tunnel vision. All you care about is the threat that you see; there is simply no brain space available to think about or consider anything else. This is important because it makes you more effective when you are running from a bear or a fire. The stress system is highly effective when there is an actual emergency.

But ... when the emergency is a deadline, a difficult colleague, three whining children while you are trying to cook dinner (sometimes just one can do the trick), or a partner who ignores your patient, repeated requests, then the emergency brain does not help but instead makes you less able to handle the situation well. In the red brain you are a faster runner and become physically stronger, so what this state is essentially telling you is to 'go harder' and it provides the energy and strength to do so. But to cope with the modern-day challenges we face on a daily basis, sheer physical strength and extra speed usually don't help. To deal with these challenges effectively, we need creativity, insight and flexibility. We need the ability to assess constantly changing situations, recognize when things are not working, and change our approach to make them work better rather than simply fall into the trap of 'go harder'.

We don't really solve a problem by going harder and longer. Instead of mindfully evaluating and changing our approach according to what we see isn't working, we keep doing the same thing with more intensity, expecting a different outcome. We fall into the myth of believing that if we work hard and are exhausted at the end, we will achieve the desired result as a natural consequence. Physical labour goals might follow this logic but mental productivity requires the opposite approach.

The red brain is the state of stress, or the emergency brain. While it works great in short-term emergencies, in long-term challenging and stressful situations, it can compromise our health, our happiness and our most important relationships.

In a red-brain state we lack control over what we think, feel and do and we are mostly driven by what our instincts tell us to do. Our stress-induced tunnel vision blocks us from seeing the bigger picture, and small insignificant problems can seem like the end of the world. Our red brain keeps us from thinking rationally, from creatively problem-solving and from learning. If the red brain is on for too long, it can impair our daily functioning.

The green brain

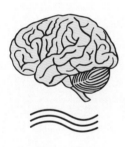

GREEN BRAIN

The green brain is the opposite of the red brain. Let me show you what happens in the green brain. Close your eyes and imagine yourself doing something that you absolutely love; something that makes you feel completely alive.

Did you notice your heart rate slowing down, your neck and shoulder muscles relaxing and your breathing becoming slower and deeper? Did you notice a sense of calmness and openness? This is the green brain or, more precisely, this is the stress hormones adrenaline and cortisol lowering and the happiness hormones oxytocin and serotonin increasing.

In the green-brain state your body works at an optimal level. You sleep well and your digestive system, immune system and sex drive all work as they should. Your emotions are balanced and you are more likely to feel happy and content, enjoying the process of things, not just the outcome. In the green brain you are at your most productive. It boosts creativity, innovation, problem-solving skills and learning. The green brain makes you caring, creates empathy and makes you feel connected to others.

The green brain is best used for everyday life when you are working, relaxing, spending time with your loved ones or even when you are doing everyday things like grocery shopping, buying a coffee or walking down the street. The green-brain state makes you notice and enjoy the little things, boosting both happiness and gratitude. For example, in the green brain I appreciate the house we live in, I am so grateful for the amazing coffee my husband makes me and I soak up all the love in the hugs my children give me. I notice the little bird by the window, I see the drive to work as a precious moment of me-time listening to my favourite music; the list could go on and on. In the green-brain state the little things stand out and make you feel grateful and happy with the life you have.

The green-brain state also makes you feel more open and connected to the people around you, which increases feelings of love and builds relationships. For example, when I'm in a green-brain state, my mornings at home are fun, even though we still have to hurry to be at school on time. All throughout the morning we are connected and the simplest activities can become moments of love. Chasing my son to put on his socks, changing my little girl's nappy as she stares at me with the biggest smile; all these small, seemingly insignificant things can be precious moments of connection, but I only notice them and engage with them when I'm in the green brain.

But when things go wrong, whether it is children who are not cooperating or a business opportunity that is about to fall through, in the green brain you can problem-solve so much better and more effectively. Instead of having tunnel vision and just continuing with your approach that isn't working, the green brain sees the bigger picture, is flexible and makes changes when things don't work.

Truly creative problem-solving only happens in the green brain. Think back to a moment when you had a great idea or came up with the perfect solution to a problem. It is not likely that this happened while you were stressing out. It is likely that you were in the green brain when the solution came to you. Or think of a big mistake you made either at work or in your personal life, something that you look back on and wish you could change. I bet you were in a red-brain state when you made that decision.

~

The red brain works hard,
the green brain works smart.

~

The green brain is the best state for everyday living and productivity. The green brain makes you flexible and creative, keeps an eye on the big picture and makes good decisions. The green brain makes everything work better (except emergencies). It brings out the most productive and happiest version of you.

The orange brain

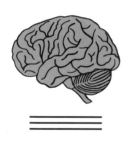

ORANGE BRAIN

On the spectrum that has the red brain at one end and the green brain at the other end, in the middle we find the orange brain. This is the brain state where we are focused on achieving. You can think of it as the 'to-do list' brain or the 'go, go, go brain'. In the orange brain we are focused on the end goal. This gives us a mild form of tunnel vision and leads us to focus only on reaching the end goal and not on the process of getting there. To put it simply, the orange brain is hiking purely to get to the top of the mountain, while the green brain is hiking for the enjoyment of the exercise and the scenery, with the end result being reaching the top of the mountain. There is nothing wrong with the orange-brain state. It doesn't have the downsides of the red brain, but it also doesn't have the benefits of the green brain. It is the neutral state — the middle ground.

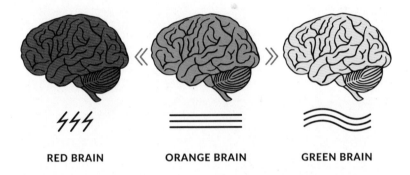

RED BRAIN   **ORANGE BRAIN**   **GREEN BRAIN**

Where you are on the spectrum doesn't depend on your situation but on your thoughts. The only exception to this rule is an emergency. For example, some people think the green brain is just for relaxation and fun, but you can be in a green-brain state while working on a challenging project either at home or at work under time pressure. This means being fully involved and focused, on top of things, innovative and smart. Can you remember a time when you were doing something challenging, something that you wouldn't consider fun, but you were fully engaged, focused and present with it? This is being productive in the green brain. These are often the times we exceed our own expectations when it comes to the quality of the work we do.

At the same time, moments we think should be green are often not green at all. You can be lying on a beach in Fiji in the red brain feeling frustrated about the hotel, the heat, the waiter, and becoming angry because the children are being too loud. In the orange brain you can be busy planning the day ahead and thinking about all the sights you want to see and all the activities you want to do and trying to make the whole family hurry up ... and not really enjoying any of it. Your brain state doesn't depend on your situation or circumstances; it depends on your thoughts. This is where mindfulness comes in.

INSIGHT QUESTIONS: BRAIN STATES

1. In which state do you spend most of your time? Are you mostly in red, green or orange?

    _____

    _____

    _____

    _____

2. Imagine what your life could be like if you lived most of it in the green brain and reserved red for emergencies only.

    _____

    _____

    _____

    _____

    _____

    _____

    _____

3. What triggers can you identify that send you straight into red brain? For example, getting stuck in traffic, IT problems or a bad cup of coffee.

    _____

    _____

    _____

    _____

    _____

    _____

INSIGHT QUESTIONS: BRAIN STATES

4. What practical changes can you make to avoid these triggers?

_____

_____

_____

_____

_____

5. When do most of your red-brain moments occur? What factors make you more vulnerable to ending up in red brain in those moments? For example, being tired or hungry or being under time pressure.

_____

_____

_____

_____

_____

6. What practical changes can you make to avoid or minimize these factors?

_____

_____

_____

_____

_____

_____

But I'm very productive in a red-brain state!

For many people it makes sense, in theory, that in the green brain everything works better, but in practice they actually get a lot more done in the red brain and the red brain helps them achieve their goals. Most people I work with have the following pattern in how they move between the brain states:

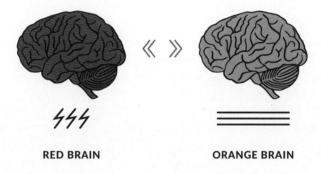

RED BRAIN   **ORANGE BRAIN**

Most people have orange as their home base, and as long as everything is going according to plan and they have everything under control, they can stay in orange. However, as soon as something goes wrong or if unexpected circumstances arise or when time pressure builds, they quickly find themselves in the red brain. In the red brain they use tunnel vision and work hard to make it to their goal so they can feel satisfied and have a brief moment of happiness.

What many people don't realize is that, while in the orange brain, they are actually spending a lot of time procrastinating and wasting time. Then, when they move into the red brain, they have a period of high stress and high productivity where they fully focus on the work they want to get done using all their energy produced by cortisol and adrenaline to finish a project, presentation or to clean the house. But because they are working from the least ideal state for productivity, it is very likely that the following will occur:

Poor time management: When you rely on stress to spark your productivity you will start the process by wasting a lot of time procrastinating. This will continue until the time pressure builds to the point that your goals are threatened. This perceived threat will induce the cortisol and adrenaline wave you need to become productive and finally focus on the goal or task at hand and then you will get to work in a panic.

Reduced enjoyment: In the orange–red productivity loop you won't be fully present nor will you really enjoy the procrastinating phase because it isn't in line with your goal. The work you have to get done will be in the back of your mind reminding you that you are not doing what needs to be done. When you reach the productivity stage the time-pressure-induced red brain will also block enjoyment of the process and your sole focus will be to reach the end result.

Tunnel vision: One of the main characteristics of the red brain is a narrow focus (keep-your-eye-on-the-bear mechanism), so tunnel vision kicks in and you only have eyes for the problem or the end goal, which makes you lose sight of the big picture and increases the potential for lesser quality outcomes. This is helpful in emergencies, but when it comes to productivity, seeing the big picture and considering all options and variables is directly linked to higher quality outcomes.

Shortcuts: In the red brain there is no 'time to think' due to time pressure so your brain takes shortcuts. When under pressure your brain reverts back to old habits and familiar ways of doing things. So shortcuts make you take the same approach you've always taken. This is not a problem if the old and familiar approach works well but, because of the complexity of the things we are dealing with in our everyday life, shortcuts may offer the fastest solution but not necessarily the *best* solution.

Less flexibility: The red brain isn't flexible because changing your approach takes up too much time. So when the chosen approach doesn't deliver the desired results, the red brain just keeps going and tries even harder, expecting a different outcome. This is why you could also call it the stupid brain. The smartest way to address lack of achievement is to realize your current approach isn't working — to pause, analyze and re-evaluate your approach to reaching your goals or to re-evaluate the goals themselves. But since all these steps take time and the red brain is all about speed, it blocks the awareness and change process, which gets you stuck in approaches that are not effective or ideal.

Poor decision-making: In the red brain state we have less brain capacity available and as a result our decision-making process suffers. Instead of carefully considering the different options and making decisions based on reason and long-term benefit, we are impulsive and make decisions based on feelings and short-term solutions. We are more inclined to go for quick fixes and are more likely to take risks and find it harder to consider long-term implications.

Energy depletion: Working from the red brain is possible but it is hard work and taxing on your brain and the rest of your body (especially your heart and adrenal glands). It depletes your system of energy rather than maintaining a healthy balance of vitality and stamina. Instead of a steady flow of energy that is sustainable and recharges itself, red-brain productivity follows a pattern of energy conservation by procrastinating followed by intense, energy-draining productivity, followed by putting the system on stand-by so the energy resources can be restored. In short, red-brain productivity goes from procrastinating to frantic productivity to collapsing in front of the TV. There is no energy left for a good conversation, a walk on the beach or a game of chess. Your brain (and the rest of your body) needs to recover its energy supply and it will put you on 'an energy conserving mode' until the energy resources are replenished.

The orange–red brain productivity loop

Orange–red brain productivity consists of a pattern that perpetuates itself. It starts with the orange brain procrastinating (conserving energy), followed by the red brain sprinting (burning all energy), followed by achieving our goal (dopamine-induced happiness), followed by the orange brain procrastinating (recovering energy), before it starts sprinting again. We don't have an unlimited reservoir of energy and when you have a habit of orange–red brain productivity, your red brain can get things done but it does so by working hard and depleting your energy resources. Your brain will balance this out with periods of conserving energy. In this pattern, your happiness is strictly linked to achieving the goal. Most of us don't really enjoy procrastinating or working intensely hard under time pressure; we do, however, enjoy the dopamine rush that comes with achieving our goal. The dopamine rush functions as a powerful reward that leads to feeling happy and satisfied — this reward system keeps this habit firmly in place, even if it isn't helpful. We got the job done so we assume our approach is working.

There is nothing wrong with this way of working but it isn't the smart, the healthy or the fun way. Basically, this approach isn't in line with how your brain was designed. The brain isn't built for going from procrastinating to sprinting to a brief moment of happiness conditional to achieving your goal back to procrastinating. It isn't in line with how people have been living for hundreds of thousands of years. It is a symptom of the times we live in and comes at a price. Long term, this way of working can lead to burnout, anxiety, insomnia, heart failure, high blood pressure and adrenal fatigue. There has to be a better way to productivity with more consistent energy and enjoyment.

The alternative to the orange–red-brain productivity pattern of *procrastination* ⟶ *sprinting* ⟶ *outcome-based reward* is the green-brain productivity loop. By switching on your green brain before you get to work, you will be able to avoid this unhelpful and unsustainable way of working and tap into a new way of being productive that reduces procrastination and gives you enjoyment of the process and the outcome. You won't feel drained or exhausted at the end and you will still get the job done. Most likely you will deliver better quality work. The green-brain productivity pattern entails *relaxing* ⟶ *focused and productive work* ⟶ *better quality outcomes*. The following tables highlight the differences between the two approaches.

Orange–red brain productivity loop

PRODUCTIVE STATE	BRAIN STATE	STRESS	HAPPINESS	ENERGY
Procrastinating	Orange	Low–medium	Reduced	Conservation
Productivity	Red	High	Reduced or no happiness	Burning all energy
Achievement	Orange (but high on dopamine)	No stress	Short-term achievement-based happiness	Out of energy

Green brain productivity loop

PRODUCTIVE STATE	BRAIN STATE	STRESS	HAPPINESS	ENERGY
Relaxing	Green	No stress	Happiness	Recharging energy
Productivity	Green (sometimes with a hint of orange)	No (or low) stress	Happiness	Using energy
Achievement	Green	No stress	Happiness	Recharging energy

As this model shows, when applied consistently, green-brain productivity can eliminate unhelpful and unhealthy stress and create more consistent energy, happiness and wellbeing.

How to shift the pattern

The first step to applying the green brain to your everyday life to boost your productivity is to identify what naturally puts you in the green zone. A lot of things naturally activate the green brain but what works for some people might not for others. Interestingly enough, our green-brain triggers are often the things that we loved doing as children. The key is to identify what your green-brain triggers are and then make sure you spend enough time each week doing them. One of the wonderful things about the green brain is that we feel great when we are in this state. Using this knowledge you can find what puts you into the green brain by asking yourself the question, 'What makes me feel alive?' In other words, what makes you feel energized, fully engaged or what is it you love to do?

Here are some of the answers people have given me when I asked them this question: painting, surfing, exercising, cooking, gardening, being around children, playing golf, sitting in a café all by myself, playing the guitar, running, working on my car, playing cards, interior design, walking the dog, hosting dinner parties, travelling, spending time with close friends, bringing dying orchids back to life, meditation, growing vegetables, doing jigsaw puzzles, reading.

We all have activities or interests that naturally put us into a green-brain state and, when you think about it, there are probably several things that do it for you. No one I know has ever answered this question with watching TV, surfing the Internet or shopping. We intuitively know the difference between the activities that give us a fleeting dopamine high or make us 'zone out' and the things that make us feel alive — things we truly love and are energized by at a deeper level.

Now you might be thinking, 'How will this make me more productive?' and that is a good question. Often it isn't during the actual green-brain activity itself that productivity increases. The activity is just a trigger to put you in the right brain state for optimal productivity for anything that follows.

The first step to having more green-brain activity in your life is to identify what activities trigger your green brain and then to make a conscious effort to get a healthy dose of those activities every week, ideally every single day. You could call it the supplements you take to keep your brain healthy. The good news is that most of the activities people come up with are completely free. The bad news is that making sure you get a healthy dose of them weekly or daily often requires setting different priorities, reorganizing your life or creative problem-solving. It's not always easy, but it is worth it.

My natural green-brain activators are being active in nature, doing things like hiking, gardening and running. Listening to music and dancing also never fails to put me in the green brain. Hugging my children is another powerful green-brain trigger and so are learning new things, writing and painting. It surprised me when I realized that as a child I already loved all of these things. As a child I was passionate about horse riding. Even though hiking, running and gardening are not the same as horse riding, they all put me in the same brain state. As a young girl I listened to music a lot and performed countless shows in front of my mirror, singing and dancing. And I loved school, learning about new things, reading, researching and then putting it on paper in my own words. This made me feel great. As a ten-year-old girl during summer break, I even wrote an essay on the galaxy just for fun. I should have realized sooner that there was a writer in me.

As an adult, these activities became completely snowed under by the business of everyday life until I finally realized there was a link between my really good productive days and the amount of time I spent doing the things I actually love. These activities used to feel like treats, things that I could do when I had spare time, when everything else was finished (it never is though!). I now see these activities as my brain vitamins. I know I need to get a healthy dose of these things daily or weekly to make sure my brain works at an optimal level. This isn't always easy but, if you make them a priority and if you go about it creatively, it can be done.

Now we start every day with the children climbing into our bed and we have morning cuddles. Then I'm off for a quick run as my husband prepares breakfast. Then, after breakfast, I turn on a song for our morning dance after which we get the children ready for school. By 8 a.m. I have already had three doses of green-brain starters: cuddles, running and dancing.

Starting your day with activities that switch on your green brain isn't just a nice way to begin the day; it is essential for productivity and success.

My way of ensuring that I start each day with my green brain 'switched on' is to combine my natural green-brain triggers with mindfulness practice. The natural green-brain activators — my brain vitamins — will automatically put me in the green zone, but mindfulness is a skill that helps me switch on my green brain anytime, anywhere.

Mindfulness

Maximizing green-brain activity and minimizing red-brain activity involves training your brain to be in the green zone through mindfulness practice. Mindfulness practice is learning a new way of thinking that activates the green-brain state, which is the first essential element for consistent productivity. Research shows that mindfulness rewires the brain and makes you better able to regulate and manage stress. In other words, mindfulness makes you better at switching on the green brain and staying out of the red brain. Mindfulness techniques use certain ways of paying attention, reshaping thoughts, breathing and posture to activate the green brain. Mindfulness stops the red brain from being triggered in situations that are not emergencies, and when you find yourself stressed, mindfulness helps you to recognize this and make your way back to the green zone.

When you successfully turn mindfulness into a habit, your brain will rewire itself and the green-brain pathways will become stronger and stronger. This makes it increasingly easier to be highly productive, not just when 'the stars are aligned' but every single day. (For an in-depth program of how to incorporate mindfulness into your life, please refer to my book *Mindfulness on the Run* and the download of my guided mindfulness techniques that can be found on my website: www.renewyourmind.co.nz.)

Morning mindfulness

My daily morning mindfulness rituals are a run and a coffee. The first five minutes of my run I spend practising mindfulness. This means nothing more than giving my full attention to my senses without allowing my mind to wander off to things that are not happening in that moment. It feels a little bit like arriving for the day, just like when you arrive at a party and you look around, scan the environment and the people there and, in a way, 'find your position'. During my mindful morning run I 'find my position' in the world around me. Every time I run I am reminded by the sound of the sea or the huge trees around me that I am so very small and dependent on nature and God. It reminds me that the cup of tea that will be spilled on the floor in ten minutes' time isn't a big deal and that the ultimate goal isn't to arrive at school exactly on time but to have a good morning together. My morning mindfulness habits help me to keep seeing the bigger picture and not get caught up in the little insignificant things.

Every morning I make sure I have a nice cup of coffee and I have at least five full minutes to drink and enjoy it. During those five minutes the cup of coffee has my full attention, the phone and laptop are out of sight and I don't allow my thoughts to wander off to everything on my to-do list. I drink my coffee mindfully and it activates and strengthens my green brain, setting me up for a good start to the day.

On a normal day, before 9.30 a.m., I have had three of my brain vitamins (morning cuddles, morning run and morning dance) and two mindfulness rituals (morning run mindfulness and mindful morning coffee). It might sound like they take up a lot of time but the truth is they take up very little time because I would be doing most of these things anyway. I am using things that are part of my usual morning ritual and have turned them into green-brain activators by bringing my awareness to them and turning them into mindful habits.

It might also sound indulgent, but I am painfully aware of the fact that without these brain vitamins and my mindfulness practice, I cannot rely on myself to be patient, kind, efficient and productive. This is what my brain needs so that I can be in control of my reactions and can create fun and loving mornings that still allow my family to be at school and at work on time. Whenever I find myself slacking off on my green-brain starters, I remind myself that this is not just for fun; it is to stop me from wasting time and to keep my productivity high. It is not just for me; it is for the health and happiness of my family as well. I want them to remember our mornings as warm, fun and without rushing and yelling, and to accomplish that I need to take responsibility for where my brain is.

It is pretty easy to do these things when I'm in a good mood and have had a good night's sleep. The challenge is to do them when I am in a bad mood and the last thing I feel like doing is dancing and singing. But the truth is that those are the days I need these rituals the most. Ideally, you take your brain vitamins every day but *especially* on the days when your brain needs a boost of health and happiness.

INSIGHT QUESTIONS: MINDFUL ACTIVITY

1. What did you love to do as a child?

2. What activities put you into the green brain now?
(Do you see the link?)

3. How much time do you spend every day, every week or every month doing these activities?

4. Could you create a daily or weekly dose of these activities?

_____

_____

_____

5. Can you incorporate some of these into your morning rituals?

_____

_____

_____

6. What are the obstacles?

_____

_____

_____

_____

_____

_____

7. How can you overcome the obstacles and make it happen?

_____

_____

_____

_____

_____

_____

_____

INGREDIENT 2:

Setting clear goals

~

*Set goals which scare and excite
you at the same time.*

~

The first ingredient to achieving healthy and fruitful productivity is switching on your green brain. The next ingredient is having clear goals. If you have clear goals but are not operating from the green brain, you will inevitably find yourself in a state of stress because you are going about achieving your goals with the least ideal brain state. You might get there in the end but you will have to work really hard and in the long run you are sacrificing your health, happiness and the quality of your most important relationships.

If you can successfully switch on your green brain you will become happier and more energized, but that might not be enough to also become more productive and successful. Turning on your green brain is like starting a car and putting it in the right gear, but if you are unclear of your destination you could be driving around aimlessly, using up precious time and fuel without having anything to show for it at the end of the day. Yes, you might have enjoyed the ride and have plenty of energy left, but there is an undeniable desire in each and every one of us for achievement, growth and to master skills. This is how our brain is wired. The need to grow is in our DNA.

Because we have this built-in desire for growth and expansion of who we are and what we want to be, we will automatically be working towards goals, even when we don't realize it. Daily goals might be to get to work on time, to cook dinner, to tidy up the house or to keep up an exercise routine. At other times our goals are simply to make ourselves feel better, to finish a work project or to undertake a business deal. Goals can also be bigger; for example, to figure out what you really what to do with your life, to find ways to make your parenting more effective, or to save enough money to buy a house. We all have goals and they drive our behaviours. If you are in the green brain, the drive will be smooth and easier; if you are in the red brain, your drive will be bumpy and (emotionally) messy, but regardless of your brain state, your goals will determine the direction.

From implicit to explicit

Our goals drive what we do from moment to moment, starting with the moment we get out of bed. Everything we do has a goal or serves a purpose. Brushing your teeth to keep them clean and healthy, drinking coffee because it helps you wake up, driving to work so you can do your job, going through the motions of your day so you get paid and can pay your mortgage — every single thing we do has a goal, even if the goal is to relax or to make ourselves feel better.

To make sure your smaller, short-term goals are driving your life in the direction that you want it to go, it is important to make your goals explicit. When you know what destination you want to arrive at in the end, you will know which pathways will help you get there. It will help you make good decisions along the way and avoid you waking up one morning and realizing you don't like your life anymore.

This doesn't mean you have to have all of your goals figured out, and it doesn't mean that you tie your overall happiness to achieving your goals. Your green brain will help you to stay connected to the journey and to enjoy the process. Setting clear goals will help determine your direction; it will guide your decision-making and help you avoid detours and distractions.

Having your goals clearly defined will also help you avoid making decisions based solely on what is comfortable. If we are not careful our brain will go on autopilot and steer us into the least challenging, most comfortable direction. Our brain has this built-in tendency to always pull us away from the unpredictable and the uncertain. It does this to help us and to try to keep us safe, even though it might not be the best course. We are at risk of getting stuck in the same loop over and over again just because it is familiar, easy and comfortable. Yes you are moving, yes you are busy, but you are not really making the progress you want. You are comfortable but comfort isn't the same as being fulfilled and happy. Often progress means stepping out, being bold and trying something new. All these things are uncomfortable but essential in personal growth. Setting clear goals will help you to stay on track with what you really want, even when the easy and comfortable options try to lure you off course.

Where
the magic
happens

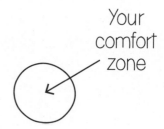

Your
comfort
zone

From big to small

Have you ever really thought about what you want your life to be like? What matters to you and how you can create a life that reflects that? It can be an overwhelming question and for a long time I didn't know how to answer it. I knew what I liked and didn't like, I knew that some things felt right and other things didn't, but formulating my life goals felt impossible until I thought about starting at the very end — literally, the end of life.

When I thought about what I wanted people to say at my funeral, it wasn't that difficult anymore. Of course, I hope they will be saying a lot of nice things and be remembering the fun times we had, but most of all I hope they say I was a good mother and partner and that my life had purpose. That I had helped many people change their lives by inspiring them and equipping them with the tools to do it. This helped me to identify and give words to what matters to me most, my biggest life goals:

» To love.
» To be a good partner and mother.
» To live a life of purpose.
» To help as many people as I can to renew their mind and live with more kind awareness.

When I started thinking about my bigger life goals, the bigger picture of what I wanted my life to be like, it was both powerful and scary. It felt both exhilarating and daunting to have my bigger life goals — the things that for me would make my life a success — written down.

The reason this is a very personal and scary process is that it moves us up one step in the process of change. It takes us from the unconsciously unskilled to the consciously unskilled. Having big goals and dreams puts the spotlight on the fact that we are not there yet and that we have a long way to go. Which is a good reminder that we desperately need our green brain to live a life of purpose. Only in the green brain can we have goals that seem impossible, yet at the same time be accepting, kind and caring towards ourselves and where we are at present. As soon as judgment and unkindness kicks in, it stalls the process towards these very goals.

Once you envisage the bigger picture — the ultimate goals made explicit and clear — it's time to narrow them down. In the end, to reach the big goals, you need to ask yourself, 'Where do I want to be ten years from now?', 'Five years from now?', 'What do I want my life to be like then?', 'What subgoals will become my stepping stones to work towards the end goals?'

To make this process more effective, you can make it not only more explicit but also more specific by focusing on different life areas. For example, when looking at my own goals, I think about what I want these life areas to be like in five years' time:

» home

» health

» mental and emotional health

» intellectual

» spiritual

» family life

» friends

» work

» finances.

After contemplating this for a while, meaning that I consciously ask myself these questions every couple of days, it leads to this goal (among other goals) for the coming five years:

To live in a beautiful and community-minded rural setting, sustainably and mortgage-free, generating a passive income and having plenty of family time. Working diversely and creatively adding value to people's lives by inspiring and equipping them with tools that rewire the brain and help them grow in kind awareness and connection to themselves and their loved ones.

If you had told me five years ago that by now this would be my goal I would have laughed in your face. It would have felt absolutely crazy and just too good to be true. And even now, when my confidence is down and anxiety gets a foot in the door, I feel exactly that. One way to get my confidence back is to remind myself that everything I have accomplished felt impossible before it was done. It *always* feels impossible and too good to be true before it is done.

Just a few years ago when I was contemplating quitting my job and starting a private psychology practice, I said to a friend, 'I just can't imagine people wanting to pay to talk to me for an hour. Who would want to do that?' Then, as my psychology practice took off and I was working long hours to meet demand, I knew I had to raise prices to make it workable and I said to the same friend, 'People want to be my clients because I am very affordable compared to other psychologists, but who will want to see me if I raise my price?' Now I feel comfortable charging more per session, but it wasn't that long ago that it simply felt impossible and too good to be true to be paid more than what I was asking at the time.

Some time ago, during a mindfulness workshop, I guided the participants through a similar exercise. I asked them to close their eyes and imagine their life ten years from now. I asked them to not hold back but to imagine it exactly the way they wanted it to be. Part of this exercise were the questions, 'Ten years from now, what sort of work do you want to be doing?' 'How do you want to feel about your work then?' 'What kind of work–life balance do you want to have?' After going through all the other life areas, I asked the participants this: 'What steps do you need to take this year/this month/this week for these goals to be achieved?'

At this point the room always becomes so silent you could hear a pin drop. Everyone has their eyes closed and for some this is the first time they have ever allowed themselves to think about the future they really want without telling themselves that what they want is ridiculous and impossible. You can see the wonder and excitement on people's faces when you create an environment that gives them permission to dare to dream. I then softly tell them, 'When you feel ready, please open your eyes and write down the steps that have come to your mind.' As people begin to write you can almost see their confidence and excitement growing. Things they deemed impossible all of a sudden begin to seem achievable and doable. As they think about the stepping stones needed to achieve the goals they first thought would be too difficult to achieve, their confidence and clarity grows.

At the end of this workshop one of the participants came up to me and thanked me for this exercise. He told me he was a graphic designer but that his passions are photography and nature. Through the exercise he realized that what he really wanted to do was become a freelance nature photographer and that he could now clearly see what steps he needed to take to make this a reality. Something that seemed impossible and too good to be true had turned into a plan with clear steps to follow. To witness this process over and over again in people is one of the highlights of my work.

This client quit his full-time job and made practical changes to his life to be able to afford to start his own freelance photography business. He now works as a freelance wedding photographer and takes tourists on photography hikes into the wilderness of New Zealand, teaching them how to take beautiful photographs of nature.

It always feels impossible until it is done

One way to boost your confidence when it comes to setting and working towards your goals is to not only pay attention to 'the gap' between where you are now and where you want to be, but to also pay attention to the 'reverse gap'. This involves reminding yourself regularly of where you were five years, three years or even one year ago and reflecting on what your life looked like then, the positive changes you have made since, what difficulties you have overcome and how you have developed and grown.

Noticing the difference between where you were a few years ago and where you are now is testimony to what you can achieve. You have accomplished things before and there is no reason to believe you cannot accomplish even bigger things now. We often forget how capable we are and what we can achieve, and simply paying attention to the reverse gap can remind us of this.

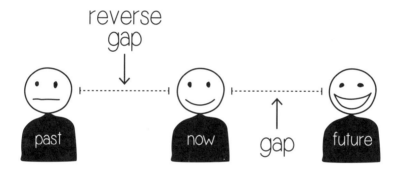

Then focus on your goals for the future again and ask yourself, 'If I want these things to become a reality five years from now, what do I have to do this month? This week? And what small step can I take today?'

The small steps

When you have identified the bigger goals that you want to accomplish, these become your WHY. Your bigger goals become the reasoning behind the small steps along the way. For example, my biggest goal is to grow in love. When I ask myself what small step I can take today to achieve that, these come to mind:

Big goal:	To grow in love.
Today's small steps:	I will treat myself to a coffee. I will make a conscious effort to smile at everyone I meet today. I will sing when I become frustrated with the kids. When the kids are in bed, I'll make Pieter a cup of tea and ask him about his day.

Why will I do these things? Because I want to grow in love. When you have your bigger picture clearly defined it helps you to make conscious and smart decisions on a daily basis. It helps you to prioritize and to say no to the things that are not a priority. For a long time I wasn't aware of what I wanted or what my 'bigger picture goal' was; I just went with the flow of what worked, what felt good and what opportunities came my way. There is nothing wrong with doing life this way, but my problem is that I like to do a lot of things and many opportunities present themselves, so as a result I would stretch myself too thin and it would tip my work–life balance the wrong way.

Having my goals clearly defined helps me to say no to things that are not the right thing or don't come at the right time. For example, one of my goals is to have my work reach as many people as possible and to have a positive impact on their lives. Yet I understand that in order to do this, and to do it well in the long term, I need to first and foremost take care of myself and my family. Therefore, being healthy and balanced myself and focusing on being a good partner and mother comes first, and in this phase of my life that is all about getting the work–life balance right.

Some time ago I was asked to speak at a Saturday event that would require me to be there for the full day and it would be on a voluntary basis. This meant I couldn't count it as a work day so the question became, 'Should I say yes or no to an extra day of fun but unpaid work that will help me spread my message but will take away a full Saturday of family time? Because at the moment I have a full workload and my number one priority is family time and realizing a good work–life balance.' The answer was that I should decline. In the past, my answer would have been yes, but my clear goals helped me to keep my priorities right and guided my decision-making.

Goals change

The beauty about goals is that they can be anything that you want them to be and you have the freedom to change them. I found that my biggest goals have stayed the same but many subgoals have changed along the way. In other words, my WHYs have remained the same but my HOWs have changed. Before my first child was born, my goal was to be a full-time mother for at least the first couple of years. But as the reality of being a full-time mother unfolded, I found out how incredibly hard it is. It took me quite some time and an understandable but pointless struggle with guilt, shame and frustration before I turned to my non-judgmental, kind awareness and came to the conclusion that full-time parenting wasn't right for me. It didn't make me happy, it didn't fulfil me, and it didn't make me the parent or the person I wanted to be.

My big goal of being a good mother stayed firmly in place but my subgoals on how to do this changed. The subgoal of being a stay-at-home mum turned into the subgoal of combining work with family in a way that does justice to both and makes me a happy mother.

Using the green brain to reach your goals

Living from the green brain as much as possible and combining it with clear goals sets you up for a new way of being productive — a productivity that is driven by purpose. Your smaller, short-term goals are your WHAT; your big long-term goals are your WHY and help you stay on track. You know why you want this and why this matters to you. This doesn't mean it will always be easy or fun. At times it will be hard and some days it will feel pointless and like it is taking forever. That is why the green brain is so essential.

To stay on track with what I really want and to keep my goals in the forefront of my mind, I start my day this way. Every day I run first down and then up a hill in a city park. As I am running down the hill I practise mindfulness, paying kind attention to the trees around me, the sounds of the birds and the flowing stream, feeling my breath and the ground underneath my feet. In this mindfulness moment I switch on my green brain. Then to further boost my green brain, I think of three small things I am grateful for. For example:

1. I am grateful for the blissful morning cuddles with my kids.

2. I am grateful for living in a beautiful place.

3. I am grateful for the dress I found in a second-hand store for only $25.

Then in the very last part of my morning run I decide on three clear goals for that day. The more specific the better. For example:

1. Between 9 and 12 I will do nothing apart from working on this book.
2. Today I will tidy the kitchen before we leave the house.
3. Today I will have my lunch at the park instead of staring at a screen scrolling through Facebook and Instagram (also known in our house as 'Wastebook' and 'Instaspam').

It takes a lot to mess up a day that started with mindfulness, gratitude and intention because it so strongly anchors you in the green brain. From there you can be aware of both the big picture and the next small step without having stress kick in. Your green brain and your goals will help you see all the good you already have and the importance of the next small step towards where you want to go.

~

Be present, be grateful and be clear
about what you really want.

~

INSIGHT QUESTIONS: GOALS

1. Think back to where you were five years ago and notice how far
    you have come since then (the reverse gap). Make a list of any
    accomplishments that come to mind.

INSIGHT QUESTIONS: GOALS

2. One way to set goals is to start with the biggest ones, asking yourself what you want to have accomplished when you die.

   What values do you want your life to encompass? What matters most to you? What do you want people to say about you when you are gone?

   _____

   _____

   _____

   _____

   _____

   _____

   _____

   _____

   _____

   _____

   _____

   _____

   _____

   _____

   _____

   _____

   _____

   _____

   _____

   _____

   _____

INSIGHT QUESTIONS: GOALS

3. To make your biggest life goals a reality, what do you want your life to be like five years from now?

   Where do you want to be living? How do you want to be spending your days? How healthy and fit do you want to be? How balanced and strong do you want to be emotionally and mentally? How do you want your intellectual and spiritual life to be? What will you be doing to create and maintain intimacy and connection with your partner? What kind of parent/uncle/aunt/friend do you want to be to the children who will be in your life?

INSIGHT QUESTIONS: GOALS

4. To make those things a reality five years from now, what small steps can you take this month? This week? Today?

_____

_____

_____

_____

_____

_____

_____

_____

_____

_____

_____

_____

_____

_____

_____

_____

_____

_____

_____

_____

_____

_____

_____

_____

_____

INGREDIENT 3:

Focus

~

*The secret of change is to focus all of your energy
not on fighting the old, but on building the new.*

— *Socrates*

~

Even when you have clear goals of what you want to be doing, actually doing what is needed for these goals to come to fruition is a different story. The things you are wanting to change in your life at the moment are probably not very different from the things you were trying to change three years ago, or maybe even ten years ago. There is a good chance that you have the same New Year's resolution each year.

The reason this happens is because we are not able to keep our focus on the goals long enough to turn them into new habits. We get lost in the daily activities, demands and ever-increasing business of life. Most of our energy and brain capacity is used by what we are doing in the present. Just keeping all the balls in the air is hard enough as it is. Adding extra things to the mix that take up more energy and attention is simply too much. So it doesn't take long before everyday life takes over and we lose focus on our goals and they begin to fade away in the background. Life isn't going to get any less busy any time soon. We also cannot expect a brain 'update' that will give us increased energy levels or improved focus capacity.

So, if we want lasting change, we have to be strategic and improve our focus on the goals we have mindfully set. Without sustained focus, goals turn into a wish list that you dream one day will magically be fulfilled. So many people treat their goals this way and there are many excuses for not following through on them: insufficient time, lack of finances, no support, etc. I believe it is a matter of focus. When you are able to keep your goals at the forefront of your mind and prevent them from slipping into the background, this stops a kind of tension called 'cognitive dissonance'. When your actions are in line with your goals, the tension is resolved and you get closer to reaching your goals, but when your actions take you further away from your goals, cognitive dissonance sets in. This is helpful because it serves as an internal alarm bell that lets you know when your behaviour is taking you further away from reaching your goals. But this internal alarm can be easily switched off as soon as we lose focus on our goals.

The power of habits

The key to keeping the focus on your goals is creating new habits. Habits are very energy efficient because they don't need your conscious focus and awareness. Habits are automated processes that work subconsciously. We all have habits but they are not all good habits. Being in control of what behaviours become habits is a huge advantage in directing your focus and reaching your goals.

When I talk about habits most people think about things like smoking, procrastinating, biting nails, gambling or overeating. But habits consist of much more than the repeated behaviours we want to change but struggle to. Almost everything you do is driven by your habits, from the moment you wake up until the moment you go to sleep. Your habits drive you almost each and every step of the way. It has been estimated that anywhere between 75 per cent and 90 per cent of what we do is habit.

Our habits kick in even before we open our eyes in the morning. Just take a moment to think about your waking-up routine. It is likely that you wake up every morning around the same time but, more importantly, you probably wake up every morning in the same way. Then, as you climb out of bed, you probably eat and drink the same things for breakfast every day, in the same order, sit on the same chair and drink out of the same cup. Then you get your things together in the same way you do every day.

It is important to realize that the habit isn't only embedded in WHAT you do but also in HOW you do it. Habits consist of repeated actions but also ways of thinking and feeling. Whether you start your day in a calm and organized or chaotic and stressed manner, it is very likely that it will be consistent day in and day out.

My waking-up habit used to be the alarm going off, hitting snooze and going back to sleep. This process would repeat itself two or three times, using the same excuses every single time: 'I'm still tired', '45 minutes should be enough time to get ready', 'Morning cuddles with my kids is important quality time' (they have a habit of crawling into bed with us every morning at 5 a.m.). In winter I would even tell myself, 'Pieter should get out of bed first to warm up the kitchen because I hate the cold.' Twenty minutes later I would drag myself out of bed, still half asleep. Because I would get up too late every single day, I always had to rush to get ready and quickly eat breakfast and organize my things for the day. The 45 minutes in my 'I want to stay in bed fantasy logic' always seemed like enough time, but it was never ever enough in my 'out of bed real life logic'. But my brain came up with clever ways to get me back in denial to make sure the habit stayed firmly in place. It convinced me that I was always rushing because of others. 'If the kids weren't all over me as I try to eat breakfast, pack my things and get dressed, I wouldn't have to rush!' or 'If Pieter would make coffee on time, my 45 minutes would be plenty of time to make it through the morning in a state of Zen'. Because of the excuses, my habit could stay firmly in place. My excuses led me to believe I wasn't causing the problem and there was no need for me to change. Of course, this is a highly unrealistic, unfair approach that allowed me to take zero responsibility for my bad morning habits. But your brain can be very convincing to protect habits and always knows just what to say to keep habits firmly in place. My morning routine didn't actually work for me. I didn't enjoy the rushing that followed the snoozing. And the truth is that it wasn't that I didn't want to change it, I simply couldn't figure out how to do it in a way that would be effective and lasting.

Understanding habits

The first step to changing your habits is to understand what they are and how they work. Your brain requires a great deal of energy to operate. When you have to concentrate or think about something, your brain's energy consumption increases drastically. When you are making decisions or solving problems you are also using up a great deal of brain energy and slowing down all the other thinking processes. This is why we say things like, 'I need a moment to think about that' or 'Let me sleep on that', and it is why we ask people in the car to be quiet when we need to figure out which lane to take on that tricky part of the motorway. We literally need time and mental space to think.

Our brain is first and foremost programmed to keep us alive and safe and an important factor in that is energy management. Your brain is programmed to use the available energy as efficiently as possible by steering you away from energy-draining processes like conscious thinking and decision-making, and increasing energy-efficient processes like habits. Simply put, habits are processes and patterns of thinking that the brain has moved from the conscious mind to the energy-saving subconscious mind, leaving more energy and conscious attention available for other things. Habits are so energy efficient because they don't require conscious thinking or decision-making; they operate on autopilot, saving us both time and energy.

This energy-saving capacity of habits is clearly shown in studies on rats learning to navigate a maze. In one particular study the researchers placed sensors on a rat's brain, then they put the rat in a very simple maze with a piece of chocolate at the end. In the beginning the rat would take ages to explore the maze, sniffing every corner, scratching the walls, walking up and down each section several times before it would find the chocolate. In the process of exploring the maze, the sensors in its brain showed constant high activity, which equals high-energy consumption in the brain. By the time the rat had done the maze several times, the exploring became less and less and each time it became quicker to get to the chocolate.

With this change in behaviour the rat's brain activity also changed. In the first couple of rounds, the brain was very active from the moment the rat was put in the maze until it had found the chocolate. After several rounds the rat became increasingly faster and the brain activity began to show a drop in activity in the middle section of each round. The experiment showed that learning is a three-stage process starting with a cue to activate the behaviour, followed by the routine, which is the behaviour itself, followed by a reward.

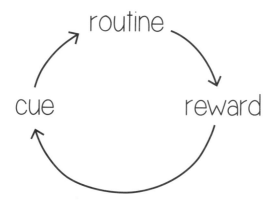

As the rat was learning the maze, its brain activity changed from consistently high to showing a drop of activity in the middle — the routine section. The brain activity would peak as soon as the rat was put in the maze, then drop as the rat was making its way to the chocolate and peak again when the rat tasted the chocolate. As the rat learned the maze, it was forming new habits. This allowed the processing of the new activity to be moved to the subconscious mind and energy consumption for the brain to be reduced. The graphs below show the brain's activity before and after a habit is formed.

First few rounds

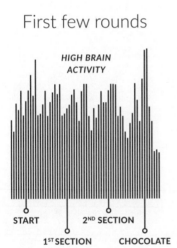

After several rounds

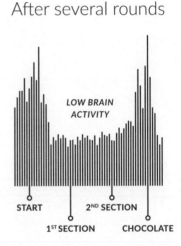

This experiment gives us a valuable peek into what happens in the brain as habits are formed. What stands out is that during the rat's drop in brain activity, the brain's energy consumption would be so low it would be similar to what it is during sleep.

The rat's brain was putting itself on stand-by mode during the entire execution of the activity — effectively 'going to sleep' and waking up again when it reached the end goal.

Humans show the same brain patterns when we form habits. Just think back to when you were learning to drive. Do you remember how intense it was? How all your senses were heightened? How you had to think about every move, from looking in the mirrors to switching on the indicator to looking over your shoulder to see what was happening in the blind spot? (I learned to drive in Amsterdam with one million bicycles around, so maybe my experience was more intense because of that!) How you needed people in the car to be quiet so you could focus on what you were doing? But after only a couple of weeks of driving you no longer needed to think about the act of driving itself; it began to happen on autopilot. As an experienced driver, you are usually able to drive somewhere on autopilot. Before you know it, you have arrived at your destination and you don't even recall the roads you took to get there.

Just like rats, when we learn behaviours we form a new habit. In the beginning it requires intense focus and concentration but when the habit is formed our brain goes on 'stand-by mode'. We get lost in thoughts, in conversation, in the song on the radio and this is only possible because we are on autopilot. Our brain has successfully automated the action so it happens subconsciously and our conscious mind is freed up to do other things.

This clever process of turning behaviours into habits that operate from our subconscious, so that brain space is freed up for other things, is essential. We would not get much done if we had to consciously think about every single thing we do. Without habits to save us energy and time we would take three hours to leave the house and be exhausted by the time we arrived at work. But sometimes our habits don't work in our favour and they can prevent us from achieving our more important goals.

Changing habits

We all know that changing habits is hard. That is why most of us have the same New Year's resolutions each year. Sooner rather than later we fall back into our old habits and then, when New Year approaches again, we come to the familiar conclusion that these old habits are not working for us and we want to change them. So we try again to turn over a new leaf, and fail again, until we simply give up. Every year my New Year's resolutions focused on exercising more, using the Internet less and doing more of what really makes me happy, like art and reading. It was only when I got so embarrassed at failing to achieve such seemingly easy goals that I stopped setting New Year's resolutions altogether.

The reason my New Year's resolutions never materialized is because I went about it the wrong way. Just like most people who want to change a habit, I focused on changing the middle part — the behaviour or routine. But the behaviour happens subconsciously, away from your control. You are pretty much sleepwalking and non-responsive when you are in this part of the habit sequence. On top of this, changing habits is the opposite of what your brain wants. Your brain wants to conserve energy and it will actively resist your efforts to change an energy-saving habit. I sometimes think of the brain as a construction manager with one of those yellow hard hats on. I call him Johnny. He and his team have been working for years to build this highly efficient network of roads (the brain's neural pathways) and then you decide, 'You know what, I'm not happy with these pathways. I want to change them into something else'. Johnny the construction manager then says, 'Are you kidding me! We've spent years building this network and now you want to change it? Hell, no! If you want to change this you are going to have to find someone else for the job!' And then he walks off mumbling to himself, shaking his head.

To top it off, changing habits requires a great deal of energy, so you are basically trying to raid the energy stores. This is a serious threat to the 'energy management people in your brain' because their job is to protect the energy stores and keep the status quo. They are armed with clever tactics to convince you that changing habits is not a good idea: 'You deserve a cigarette, you've worked so hard', 'Why would you get out of bed where it is warm and soft and blissful just to go running outside where it is cold and dark?', 'It is so unfair to deprive yourself of the one thing that makes you feel better, so go on and open that bar of chocolate. This time you will only have one piece.'

The things your brain comes up with to keep its energy-saving systems safe include lies, lures and sweet talks to get you back into your old habits. I sometimes feel like I have an inner politician swaying me with lies that sound like truths and it feels like I have no defence. Which is actually true; you have no defence because the very nature of the habit is that the routine part of it happens in your subconscious where you have no control.

To sum up, when you are trying to change a habit by changing the routine, the behaviour part of the habit fights against you. This is because the routine part happens at the subconscious level, which is equivalent to sleepwalking, and second of all because your brain actively resists your attempts to raid its energy supply to change a habit that, from an energy-saving perspective, works just fine. Changing habits is a classic example of how your brain is programmed for survival and efficiency, not for happiness and fulfilment. Even when you can muster up the motivation and willpower to go against your brain's advice and change the habit, most of us will slip back into it within a couple of weeks, before the new behaviour has been around long enough to form a new habit.

However, most of us will have the experience of successfully changing a bad habit at some point in our lives. Since I started practising my mindfulness techniques on a daily basis (as described in the book *Mindfulness on the Run*), I have successfully changed the following bad habits:

- » worrying about finances
- » worrying about time
- » harsh and critical self-talk
- » working too much
- » self-doubt
- » becoming overwhelmed with the kids
- » snapping at my loved ones.

All of these habits are stress-related and I was able to change them because mindfulness is part of my daily habits. But there were more non-stress-related bad habits that I wanted to change — things that were much harder to stay focused on and every time I would lose direction and slip back into my old habits before the new changes could become second nature.

Changing habits strategically

We are able to change bad habits if we understand how they operate. We need to be strategic about keeping our focus on the new behaviours long enough for them to become habits. A great way to get started is to do a 'mindful life edit'.

Mindful life edit

The first step in changing a habit is to apply your conscious awareness and figure out what it is you want to change. The routine part of the habit operates at a subconscious level, out of reach of your conscious mind and willpower. Therefore, step one in successfully changing habits is to bring them into your awareness, into your conscious mind, where you have more control. New Year's resolutions are a perfect example of this process of consciously paying attention to your life and identifying the things that don't work for you anymore. But you don't have to wait until December to do a life review of what habits you want to change. You can do it right now.

To begin, first focus on what is working by simply asking yourself, 'What is working well in my life?' Write everything down that comes to mind. When you have identified what is working for you, I suggest you give yourself the freedom to be absolutely stoked about what is working well. The more excited you can be about what is working well, the more energy you will have to help change the things that are not working well.

Next you need to focus on 'What isn't working for me?' Pay attention to what isn't working with kindness, without judging it. Kindness is essential because emotions such as guilt, shame, frustration and sadness just get us more stuck in these unhelpful behaviours and make them even harder to change.

Next, pick one thing on your 'What isn't working well?' list and ask yourself, 'What would help?' Your mindful attitude will activate your green brain, which you then put into problem-solving mode. You will notice that as soon as you ask yourself this question, new ideas and insights will pop into your mind. Don't judge the ideas but write down everything that comes to mind, even if the ideas are unrealistic and impossible. The goal isn't to have good ideas but to have many ideas — the more ideas, the better. If you write them down they will begin to unfold further and, even though not everything you will come up with will be helpful, this process can generate some real gems that you hadn't thought of before.

When you have a long list of ideas, circle the ones that you think might actually work and try them out.

The first thing this exercise accomplishes is that it allows you to see that even though there are things that aren't working, there will also be a lot of things that are working. It's easy to lose sight of everything that is going well and take it for granted. The simple act of writing a list helps us to notice all the things that we have to be happy about. The second thing it helps us do is pay kind, conscious awareness to what isn't working well. We don't often stop to think about what in our life isn't working well. We spend plenty of time worrying about it, feeling frustrated about it and complaining about it, but we don't often stop and really think things through.

This exercise has been a game changer for me and it has helped me solve some big and some small problems (see opposite). For example, at one point I was really struggling to make time to work on my first book, so my pick from the list of what wasn't working well was 'book writing': I can't find time to write the book without compromising work or family time. Then I started the idea generation process and I wrote down everything that came to mind. In reality, the list was much longer than this, but it covered the same themes.

Most of the ideas I came up with were unrealistic and impossible, but the goal wasn't to have only *good* ideas, the goal was to have *many* ideas. From an unrealistic idea, 'I could write at night' came a not so unrealistic idea, 'I could write early on weekend mornings.' In the past I had experienced

INSIGHT QUESTIONS: LIFE EDIT
(SAMPLE)

1. What is working well?

   Eating healthy

   Mindfulness routine

   Stress management is pretty much under control

   Morning routine (most days at least)

2. What isn't working well?

   (Book writing)

   Exercise routine

   Dinner routine

3. What would help?

   I could stop writing the book.

   I could get someone else to write it for me.

   I could make it a really short book.

   I could write instead of seeing my clients.

   I could take three months off work and write it then.

   I could hide in a cabin in the woods for a week and
   have uninterrupted writing time.

   I could write at night.

   I could write early on weekend mornings!

INSIGHT QUESTIONS: LIFE EDIT

1. What is working well?

_____

_____

_____

_____

_____

2. What isn't working well?

_____

_____

_____

_____

_____

3. What would help?

_____

_____

_____

_____

_____

_____

_____

_____

_____

_____

_____

that if I had to I can be very productive early in the morning. So I decided to give it a try. For about six months I got up early every Saturday and worked on the book from 6 to 9 a.m. It didn't take anything away from my work time and I still had nearly the whole day to spend with my family. Without doing this exercise and thinking this problem through with conscious awareness, I probably would never have thought of this solution. It worked brilliantly and *Mindfulness on the Run* was completed six months later.

Sometimes applying the ideas that pop up in the 'What would help?' section is enough to shift what is needed for lasting change. Sometimes your brain needs a bit more help.

Find your WHY

Another tool in changing habits is setting a clear goal and identifying your strongest WHY. The example overleaf sets out how to do this.

When you are being hypnotized into an old unhelpful habit, your strongest WHY can serve as your 'wake-up trigger'. Reminding yourself of your WHY can snap you out of autopilot mode because it reminds you of the importance of the change. It reminds you of what you really want:

» I want to eat that chocolate cake, but I want to be healthy even more.

» I want to snooze, but I want a fun morning with my family even more.

» I want to browse online, but I want to go home early even more.

» I want to complain about my work, but I want to be positive and feel good even more.

» I want to zone out and watch TV, but I want to feel fulfilled by reading a good book even more.

INSIGHT QUESTIONS: FIND YOUR WHY
(SAMPLE)

1. What do I want to do?

   I want to run every morning instead of snoozing.

   _____

   _____

2. Why is that important to me?

   Because snoozing just makes me more tired.

   Snoozing always turns into rushing.

   Because I want to have great energy.

   I want to get in shape.

   I want to start the day active and in the green brain.

   I want the mornings to be rush-free and filled with

   fun family time (they are not fun when I'm rushing!).

INSIGHT QUESTIONS: FIND YOUR WHY #1

1. What do I want to do?

2. Why is that important to me?

INSIGHT QUESTIONS: FIND YOUR WHY #2

1. What do I want to do?

   _____

   _____

   _____

   _____

   _____

2. Why is that important to me?

   _____

   _____

   _____

   _____

   _____

   _____

   _____

   _____

   _____

   _____

   _____

   _____

   _____

   _____

   _____

   _____

Sometimes having your WHY clear and explicit is enough to not give in to temptations and instead do what you want to be doing even more. Sometimes you need a bit more help in finding effective ways to change the unhelpful routines.

Write down your goals and all the reasons why that goal matters to you. Then circle the reason that matters most to you and you will discover your most important WHY.

How to achieve your goals

From the WHAT and the WHY we move on to the HOW. *How* will you achieve your goals?

To be strategic about the HOW means to work with the cues and the rewards that present themselves rather than just trying hard to change the behaviour itself. The cues and the rewards work when your brain is online and responsive. Therefore making changes is more likely to be successful when you pay attention to them.

The first step is to identify the cue that activates the habit. The cue is usually the thing that happens right before the habit kicks in. Cues can be surroundings, actions, thoughts or feelings. The cue functions as Pavlov's bell.

Ivan Pavlov was a famous Russian psychologist who, among other things, studied what we call classical conditioning, which is an automatic and subconscious form of learning. Like many great scientific discoveries, Pavlov discovered classical conditioning by accident. In the 1890s, Pavlov was studying the salivation responses of dogs that were being fed. He noticed that after a short time, the dogs would begin to salivate as soon as he entered the room, even when there was no food in sight.

Pavlov studied this phenomenon further and found that any object or event that the dogs learned to associate with food would trigger the salivation response as well. In this process, a stimulus that beforehand was neutral was given learned meaning by linking it to something else. For example, during one of Pavlov's experiments, he would sound a bell every time the lab dogs were fed. In the beginning the bell was neutral; sounding the bell didn't lead to any particular response in the dogs. But after only a couple of times of sounding the bell when the dogs were given their food, just hearing the bell would be enough for the dogs to start salivating. The bell being paired with the food had become the conditioned cue. As soon as the dog heard the bell, its body would automatically get ready for the food, even when there was no food in sight.

Pavlov found that for this type of learning to occur, the stimuli need to be present close together in time. Our habits are also conditioned and the cues set them in motion.

For example:

Cue: Alarm going off.
Behaviour: Snoozing.

Cue: Sitting down at your desk and checking emails at the end of a workday.
Behaviour: Wasting time on Facebook.

Cue: Sitting down on the sofa and turning on the TV when you come home.
Behaviour: Ordering takeaway food when you have vegetables in the fridge.

Remember that the cues automatically set off the habit; it is the cue that 'hypnotizes' you into the behaviour. If you can avoid the cue, you will have more control over what you do.

For example:

Habit: Snoozing.

Cue: Alarm going off.

Avoiding the cue: Change the alarm tune (even better, also change the location of the bed or the room where you sleep in for a while until the new habit has been established).

Habit: Wasting time on Facebook.

Cue: Feeling tired after the last meeting of the day and sitting down at your desk to check emails.

Avoiding the cue: After the last meeting, don't sit down to check your emails but mix it up. Check your emails standing up or in the car. Even better, don't check your emails but instead talk to someone, make yourself a cup of tea, anything but sitting down at your desk.

Habit: Ordering takeaway instead of cooking a healthy meal.

Cue: Sitting down on the sofa and turning on the TV when you come home.

Avoiding the cue:	When you come home turn on the radio instead of the TV and avoid sitting down. If you can, start cooking straight away or simply take the vegetables out of the fridge so they are in sight while you do something else.

A commonly asked question by parents, especially those who have teenagers, is: 'How can I reduce my child's screen time?' Technology is highly, highly addictive and the cues are everywhere. Most families have more screens than actual family members and often they are given prominent places in the house so they are always in sight, making them powerful visual cues. If your child has a habit of looking at a screen more than you think is healthy, you need to remove the triggers — remove the cues. Take the screens out of sight so they don't get triggered into the habit constantly. If you are scrolling on your phone instead of talking to your partner before you go to sleep, leave the phone in the kitchen. If your teenager is texting his friends during dinner, make a rule that everyone puts their phone in a drawer when it is dinnertime. If your toddler has a tantrum when she isn't allowed to watch TV, put a blanket over the TV so it isn't functioning as a magnet as much. Remove the visual cues and avoid double standards; you cannot expect your teenager to be excited about reading a book when you are sitting next to her on the sofa working on a laptop.

~

*A good way to change a bad habit is
to replace it with a good habit.*

~

Recently I worked with a client who had a habit of comparing herself to others and focusing on all the things other people had that she didn't. The result of this focus on what she was 'lacking' was that she frequently felt stressed, down and inadequate. After some exploring, we found that the low moments of her day often happened right after she had been on a break, when she would go on social media and look at other people's posts. Feeling down after her breaks made perfect sense because her habit of scrolling through her social media feed had become a cue that would set into action the habit of comparing herself to others. One solution to this problem was to avoid the cue. She took a week-long break from social media and noticed that in just a week she felt less down and more happy with her life and herself. During this week, I also asked her to write in a journal three things she felt grateful for every time she felt the urge to go on social media. In this process she didn't just stop the bad habit, she replaced it with a new healthy one. She changed a habit that made her feel inadequate to one that boosts her confidence and makes her feel strong and capable.

In some situations the cue that sets off an unhelpful habit cannot be avoided. If this is the case, it can be helpful to ask yourself what is the purpose of the unhelpful habit and if there is a more helpful habit that can replace it. For example, I worked with a ten-year-old boy who had got stuck in a long and detailed bedtime routine in which he had to go to the bathroom five times, shake up his pillow seven times and position all his toys in a certain way. The root of the problem was anxiety, which he was able to keep at bay throughout the day as he was busy and had other things to focus on, but in the evening when he would go to bed and everything became quiet the anxiety would come out. His rituals were a way of calming the anxiety, however he became stuck in the rituals and needed more and more of them to be able to go to sleep. For this little boy, going to bed had become a cue to the anxiety surfacing and that had become a cue that activated the unhealthy habit of rituals.

As most parents would, his parents tried their best to help him to reduce the rituals but with little success. The cue of going to bed and needing peace and quiet to fall asleep isn't something we can avoid. The goal of the rituals was to reduce his anxiety so instead we worked on replacing the unhelpful bedtime ritual with a helpful one in which he did calming mindfulness techniques together with one of his parents. This way, the bedtime quietness became paired with anxiety-reducing mindfulness that he would do together with a parent. Bedtime changed from being something he would dread to something more positive. It went from an anxiety-filled process to a connected and empowering process in which he learned he could do something about his anxiety in a more helpful way.

Rewards

Just like the cue, the reward 'wakes up your brain'. Because of this the reward is another powerful tool in changing habits that are no longer working for you. People often underestimate the power of rewards and therefore don't utilize their potential. The truth is that we are all driven by rewards; they are part of our nature. Our brain is wired to seek rewards because they release the chemicals dopamine, serotonin or oxytocin in our brain. These chemicals make us feel good and as a natural result we seek more of the things that triggered them. Knowing this, you can strategically use rewards to help you build and strengthen more helpful habits to replace the unhelpful ones. For example, if you want to take up a habit of running and you give yourself a small piece of chocolate after every run, you will be more likely to turn running into a new habit. If you want to get into the habit of tidying up the house before you sit down and get to work (I work from home most days), postpone your coffee until after you have tidied up. If you

INSIGHT QUESTIONS: CHANGE A HABIT #1

1. What habit do you want to change?

2. What cues precede the behaviour you want to change?

   Cues can consist of location, time of day, mood or actions (among other things).

3. How can you avoid the cues?

   When you have identified the cues, try to change them simply by mixing things up.

INSIGHT QUESTIONS: CHANGE A HABIT #2

1. What habit do you want to change?

_____

_____

_____

_____

_____

2. What cues precede the behaviour you want to change?

   Cues can consist of location, time of day, mood or actions (among other things).

_____

_____

_____

_____

_____

_____

3. How can you avoid the cues?

   When you have identified the cues, try to change them simply by mixing things up.

_____

_____

_____

_____

_____

want to stop smoking, go and chat to your colleagues in the lunchroom when you normally would have a cigarette.

A reward can be anything that you like (and can get addicted to). It can be sugary foods, socializing, watching a funny video or going outside for a walk. What is a reward for one person could be more like a punishment for another. My husband rewards himself by going to the gym. I couldn't think of anything worse! Finding out what makes you feel good will help you find potential rewards you can use to strengthen the new habits.

As I mentioned earlier, changing a habit isn't so much about stopping the habit as it is about replacing it with something else — something more helpful, something healthier. You don't have to choose between the broccoli and the chocolate. Instead use the chocolate to reward yourself for eating the broccoli and you might find that in time you won't enjoy eating the chocolate as much.

When I started running in the mornings, one of the obstacles I had was finding my running gear. When I noticed this obstacle I started putting my running clothes and shoes by the front door in the evening. This simple change to the routine removed an obstacle and created a new cue (seeing my running gear by the front door) to help reinforce the new habit.

What new habit do you want to create?

On page 92, write down the new habit you want to create. Think about how can you reward yourself for doing the new behaviour. Examples of rewards are food, drinks, social interaction, doing something fun or positive self-talk.

What are the obstacles?

Old habits die hard so we need all the help we can get. One way to ensure your success is to think about the obstacles and be strategic about them. For example, obstacles can be time, organization, finances or other people. Thinking about the obstacles beforehand means that you can enter the challenge with a plan and you won't be caught by surprise and defeated. Paying attention to the hiccups along the way will show you where the unexpected obstacles are so you can be strategic about them too.

How can you work around the obstacles?
What would help?

After you have identified the obstacles, repeat the idea-generating exercise at the beginning of this chapter. Ask yourself, 'How can I work around them?', 'What would help?', and write down any ideas that come to mind. Try not to judge them but to let your imagination run wild and think outside the box. When you have a long list of ideas, circle the ones that might work for you and try them out.

INSIGHT QUESTIONS: A NEW HABIT #1

1. What new habit do you want to create?

   _____

   _____

   _____

   _____

2. How can you reward yourself for doing the new behaviour?

   (For example, food, drinks, social interaction, doing something fun or positive self-talk.)

   _____

   _____

   _____

   _____

3. What are the obstacles?

   _____

   _____

   _____

4. How can you work around them? What would help?

   _____

   _____

   _____

   _____

   _____

   _____

INSIGHT QUESTIONS: A NEW HABIT #2

1. What new habit do you want to create?

2. How can you reward yourself for doing the new behaviour?

   (For example, food, drinks, social interaction, doing something fun or positive self-talk.)

3. What are the obstacles?

4. How can you work around them? What would help?

INGREDIENT 4:

Energy

~

Cherish and nurture your body and brain.
They are your most precious possessions.

~

Energy is the ingredient that enables the brain to be productive, just like petrol is the fuel for the engine enabling a car to drive. But we can't just pull over at a brain energy station to fill up our tank (even though some of us try to mimic that effect through drinking coffee).

People rightfully associate great energy with a good mood, high productivity and motivation. When we have great energy, we get stuff done and we feel fantastic because of it. When we have great energy, we can be creative in our problem solving and stay in touch with the bigger picture of our goals and values, even when things go wrong. Most of us will also intuitively feel that having great energy will have a positive impact on relationships, self-esteem and ageing.

Having great energy begins with understanding what supplies us with the energy we need, what drains energy from our system, and how we can make changes to either increase energy production, reduce energy 'leakage' or a combination of both to achieve stress-free productivity.

Energy sources

The easiest way to understand what supplies us with the energy we need is to look at the world around us. Take plants, for example. What do plants need to grow? Plants need nutrients, which they get from healthy, nutrient-rich soil. Plants also need fresh air, plenty of sun and clean water. Our make-up isn't that different from plants in the sense that we also need real, nutrient-rich food, plenty of sun, fresh air and clean water. The simple formula that applies is that the quality of the input determines the quality of the output.

Food

In the last 50 years or so, our diet has changed drastically. How our food is produced, processed, stored, packaged and prepared has dramatically altered. These changes to our diet mean that what we consume daily is very different in its nutritional content from that which even our closest ancestors consumed.

The food and grocery system has evolved a great deal and is able to supply most of us in the western world with food, but in some cases it has been a matter of quantity over quality. Some things we consider to be food are actually artificially engineered products that have been given some attractive labels such as 'fat-free', 'diet' or 'sugar-free'. It has been estimated that the average person in industrialized countries will eat more than 4 kg (9 pounds) of additives every year. The impact of this on our physical and mental health is still largely unknown, as governments have appeared reluctant to fund, conduct or publish rigorously controlled studies examining the effects of additives.

There is growing evidence that diet plays an important contributory role in specific mental health problems, including attention deficit hyperactivity disorder (ADHD), depression, schizophrenia and Alzheimer's disease. A balanced mood and feelings of wellbeing can be protected by ensuring that our diet provides adequate amounts of complex carbohydrates, protein, essential fats, amino acids, vitamins and minerals and water.

Most of us know that fast food isn't good food, but because we are time poor, preparing a real, nutrient-dense dish takes more time then picking up a takeaway or microwaving a frozen supermarket meal. One of the things that helped me build up the motivation to change from eating quick meals and doing a whole lot of snacking to eating a real, nutrient-dense diet was simply focusing on the goal. I wanted to feel better and have more energy, so I reassessed the fuel I was putting into my body every day and changed the way I ate. It just made sense. A mantra that helped me stay on track was:

~

Eat well, feel well.
(goal + why)

~

It is common sense, backed up by science, that if you eat well you feel well. One study done with young female adults showed that just ten days of eating a nutrient-dense Mediterranean diet gave them significant improvements in self-rated vigour, alertness and contentment. When you eat well you will have more energy, a better mood and find it easier to be proactive and productive.

Another obstacle that I found when I was in the process of changing my diet was cost. Organic, real food is expensive and often I thought it was too expensive but I never stopped to think how much the cookies, chocolate, potato chips and other snacks I ate on a daily basis cost. Adding it all up, I spend nothing more on my organic, nutrient-dense diet than I did on my fast food and snacks diet. Plus I will be saving a lot on healthcare costs along the way. I now live by:

~

I cannot afford to eat bad food;
it costs me my energy, mood,
productivity and money.

~

Eating real food in a fast-paced society is a real mission. It takes planning and time to cook, but it can be done. Taking small achievable steps in the right direction and making it fun is the way to go. Visit farmers' markets, buy a beautiful cookbook, ask your friends for their favourite recipes, start by changing just one of your main meals. Remember to take it one step at a time.

Water

Drinking clean water and plenty of it is another essential element in supplying your body with what it needs to create great energy. We all are naturally thirsty but it is so tempting to go for sweet, artificial or caffeinated drinks instead of pure water. And, even trickier, most water that runs out of taps isn't that clean. It can be contaminated with aluminium, arsenic and copper among many other things, and often chemicals have been added to make it 'drinkable'. Investing in a good water filter helps to get rid of some of the most harmful chemicals added to common tap water.

There are also some practical things you can do to ensure you drink enough water to supply your body with what it needs. Keep a water bottle with you at all times. Make sure you are using one that is intended for refilling; if you use thin plastic water bottles, make sure they are BPA-free to reduce any health risks.

Then make it taste great! Add some basil, cucumber, lemon, fresh mint or even strawberries for a delicious flavour. You could also try out different hot and cold teas. It is amazing to notice how quickly your taste changes back to how it was intended to be, and before you know it you will find sweet, sugary drinks way too sweet.

Sun

The sun has got a bad reputation over the last couple of years, partly due to high rates of melanoma. Melanoma is an aggressive form of skin cancer and a serious issue. However, the approach of avoiding the sun totally might be doing more harm than good. We need to remember to avoid getting sunburned at all times, but assuming you don't need any sun exposure at all is also dangerous. Our bodies are designed to be exposed to the sun, and totally covering up with clothes or sunscreen at all times blocks the natural sun from providing our bodies with the energy we need. Vitamin D is called the sunshine vitamin for good reason. A lack of sunlight can lead to a vitamin D deficiency; a health problem that several researchers believe 50 per cent of the world's population is at risk of developing. Vitamin D deficiency has also been linked to autoimmune diseases, infectious diseases, cardiovascular disease and several types of cancers.

Noticing that the plants in my garden that only get a little sun don't die but also don't flourish is a gentle reminder of my sun mantra:

~

Sunshine is like coffee:
don't burn it and don't run out.

~

Research shows that the required daily dose of sunlight depends on many factors, including skin colour, weather conditions, latitude, altitude and even the time of day. An online calculator will show you how much time you need to spend in the sun to maintain optimum vitamin D levels depending on where you live. Know your body, and if you easily burn in certain areas, make sure you cover them.

Air

Another underestimated source of energy is fresh air. Fresh air gives our lungs the opportunity to get toxins out of the body and recharge our system with good-quality oxygen. So many of us work in buildings where you can't open the windows and an air filtration system is the only way to get fresh air into the building. These systems create a tightly sealed bubble with sometimes hundreds of people in it, with just one 'straw' pumping in a tiny amount of fresh air throughout.

Reduced air quality and a lack of oxygen impact the brain by impairing concentration, focus and cognitive functioning. It also causes fatigue and low mood. Simply opening windows to allow air to flow ensures your office or home will have plenty of fresh air. If this isn't possible because of the building you work or live in, make sure you take regular breaks and go outside to fill your lungs with fresh air.

Looking at life's basic organisms can teach us simple, yet valuable lessons on what we need to have great energy. However, humans are not plants and our needs are more complicated than those of plants. If we move up the chain to a life form that resembles us even more than plants, we can learn even more about what fuels our energy on a daily basis.

Animals

Humans fall under the category of mammals, and other mammals resemble us in many ways. In fact, some species have up to 99 per cent of the same genes as us! So looking at how mammals function, and what gives them energy, can give us more insight into what we need for great energy.

Sleep

One of the most basic sources of energy is sleep. We all know that a good night's sleep works wonders for clear thinking, mood, energy and spirit and that having to plough through a day when you have had a broken night feels like a continuing nightmare.

During sleep your brain gets busy. Sleep is a brilliantly designed solution for one of the brain's most basic needs — to be cleaned. Yes, that's right, your brain needs to be cleaned and that's exactly what happens when you go to sleep. All our organs, including the brain, need oxygen and fuel (nutrients) to function. A byproduct of our functioning organs is waste.

The body's central nervous system consists of the brain and the spinal cord, which contains cerebrospinal fluid. This clear liquid surrounds the brain and spinal cord and moves through a series of channels called the glymphatic system, which surrounds the brain's blood vessels. This system is responsible for the brain's cleaning duties. It collects the brain's waste and dumps it into the bloodstream so it can be disposed of. However, the brain has its own unique approach to housekeeping — the cerebrospinal fluid only flows through the brain when you are asleep.

The brain optimally uses all the space it has in the skull and somewhere in the design process it was decided that adding an active waste disposal system alongside the nutrient supply system (like the rest of the body) would take up too much space. It would give us disproportionately big heads. So Nature came up with this brilliant and unique way of cleaning the junk from our brains that kicks into action when we sleep.

When you go to sleep your brain shrinks by 60 per cent. It is then that the cerebrospinal fluid is flushed through the brain, along the outside of the blood vessels, to collect the waste sitting between the cells and then dump it into the bloodstream. You could compare it to you and your family members not doing any cleaning or tidying throughout the day and then, when you are all asleep, a cleaning crew comes in and tidies up and collects all the rubbish, dust and dirt and puts it on the sidewalk to be collected by the night-time garbage truck. Isn't that amazing! Honestly, I would hire a night-time cleaner in a heartbeat! Just imagine waking up in the morning to discover the whole house was cleaned while you were fast asleep!

This process of your brain cleaning itself when you are asleep works perfectly as long as you are sleeping well. If you have trouble sleeping on a regular basis, your brain might begin to look like my house when I'm working on a book. The laundry piles up, there are cups and plates in random places, and I don't bother tidying up the toys because I tell myself, 'What's the point? They will be all over the floor again in five minutes.' Needless to say, if I stopped cleaning, it wouldn't be long before our house became unliveable. This is what happens to your brain when you don't get enough sleep, or when you don't get good-quality sleep over a long period of time. You can still function with a brain that has some dust and a full laundry basket, but if the problem persists and the junk starts to pile up, you will end up with a dirty brain that doesn't function properly.

Several things happen when you don't get enough good sleep over a period of time.

Physical health problems: First of all, lack of sleep negatively impacts the immune system and decreases the amount of white blood cells in your body. Because your immune system is the one and only thing your body has to fight viruses, bacteria and restore damage, a lack of sleep has been linked to a wide variety of health issues, including heart disease, obesity, infections, diabetes and cancer. Studies done by teams from the University of Chicago and the University of Louisville show that interrupted sleep can speed cancer growth, increase tumour aggressiveness and reduce the immune system's ability to fight early cancers.

Mental health problems: How we sleep impacts how we feel. Studies show that bad sleep correlates with depression, anxiety and burnout. One study showed that people with insomnia are ten times more likely to also have clinical depression and seventeen times more likely to have an anxiety disorder. Not sleeping well and feeling down or anxious go hand in hand and perpetuate each other.

Cognitive functioning and productivity: When you don't sleep well your dirty brain struggles to do the things you want it to do. Studies show that insomnia impairs attention, concentration, memory and problem-solving, and it decreases productivity significantly, especially in routine tasks.

Movement

Another basic element for great energy is movement. Being physically active uses energy but also gives energy. Many of us get out of bed in the morning, sit down at the kitchen table to eat our breakfast, drive to work, park the car in the office basement, take the elevator to the office just to sit down behind our computers for the rest of the day. After a day of work we go through the exact same process but replace breakfast with dinner. Then if we're unlucky, we will spend our evening staring at our laptop doing more work from home. If we're lucky we'll spend the evening staring at the TV or browsing, pinning or liking on social media. Even chores such as grocery shopping, buying books, clothes and presents can all be done online now and trips to the shops have become obsolete. It is becoming more and more challenging to get our much-needed movement.

A lack of physical activity increases the risks of obesity, cardiovascular disease, impaired cognitive functioning and cancer. There are also strong links between inactivity and depression. Whether we like it or not, to be healthy, all of us need to be moving. Our bodies were simply not made to sit still behind a device all day.

The good news is that you don't have to become a gym bunny to get your daily dose of movement. Simple changes such as taking the stairs, parking a block away from your destination and walking the rest of the way, walking during your breaks or to meetings and finding fun ways to exercise make it a bit easier to get your daily dose of movement.

Personally, I don't like going to the gym at all. I love how I feel after a gym session, but I find it pretty boring. Plus the time investment, organizing and planning my other activities around it just make it too much of a chore. When I started on a mission to change my sleep routine, changing my morning routine became part of the plan. I took up a habit of running first thing in the morning and started with just five minutes. This way I could get in some exercise without having to plan, organize or invest a lot of time, plus it helped me wake up, warm up and be productive in the early hours of the day. I also love hiking and as a family we made a plan to do a long hike every weekend. Within a few weeks I began to love my morning run. I was amazed at how much energy it gave me and how much time it saved through the increase in productivity in the morning. Remember, small steps can create big results.

Relationships

Mammals (and many other animals) need relationships to survive and thrive. If an animal is excluded from the pack it will perish. Studies show that monkeys who are excluded from their troop usually die within a year. This used to be the same for us humans. Some time ago, our survival depended on being accepted and protected by the group we belonged to. Because of this recent history we still have strong emotional reactions to being rejected or excluded. Our brain is wired to make rejection and exclusion emotionally painful because it drives us to do our very best to prevent it, hence ensuring the best chances for survival.

Nowadays, relationships might not be essential for survival, but they remain essential for wellbeing. Research shows that the number of close relationships you have, whether it is with a partner, friends or family, accurately predicts your health and happiness, and being isolated and lonely impacts health and happiness dramatically.

Loneliness is one of the western world's biggest psychological problems, often disguised as depression and addictions, including work addiction. Being lonely might not kill you, but it does suck the life out of you and depletes your energy and zest for life. If you have ever felt lonely you know how deeply this impacts people and if you have great relationships you will know how spending an evening of quality time with a friend can 'fill up' your energy tank.

Loneliness is on the rise and not just in old people. Many people suffer from loneliness without even realizing it, and social media plays an important role in this. According to a 2016 Nielsen social media report, adults between 35 and 49 years of age spend almost seven hours per week on social media followed by millennials, who spend close to six hours per week on social media. According to a Common Sense Media report, teens between the ages of thirteen and eighteen are spending around nine hours a day on entertainment media and children aged eight to twelve spend about six hours a day doing the same.

I believe it is safe to say that most people you know, perhaps yourself included, suffer from a social media addiction. The rise in loneliness and an increase in the ability to connect with people online only makes sense if you understand how the brain processes social media. Checking your email, text messages, Facebook, Instagram, Pinterest, WhatsApp, Snapchat or any app works as social junk food for your brain. Every time you scroll through your social media feed, you are snacking on social junk food.

When you eat junk food your body reacts in the same way as it would if you were eating real food. It gives signals of appetite, it produces saliva, happy chemicals are released that give you the experience of enjoying the food, and when you have eaten a certain amount it will give you the signal that you are full. Because junk food mimics the properties of real food, it tricks your body into responding as if you have just eaten a real meal. The problem is that what you have eaten has little nutritional value. The whole purpose of eating is to provide your body with fuel. When you eat junk food instead of eating something your body can use for fuel, you end up starving yourself due to consuming very few nutrients even though you feel full.

Social junk food works the same way. Your brain naturally drives you to want to connect socially and to be interested in social information because it helps keep you safe by staying connected to the group. In other words, your brain is naturally hungry for social interaction and validation. When this hunger is satisfied by scrolling, liking and texting, you are tricking your brain into thinking it has received real, meaningful social interaction. The happy relationship chemicals serotonin and oxytocin are released and you feel satisfied. However, just like with junk food, you haven't had real, reciprocal connection at all, the kind that fosters relationships and gives energy. By replacing real, meaningful social interaction with social junk food, you are satisfying your natural appetite for connection without ever receiving it. This lack of real connection leads to an increased risk of loneliness. To reduce the loneliness, your brain will drive you to connect even more. If you do this by giving yourself another social media hit, you will feel better in the short term but even worse long term — your feelings of loneliness will grow. This is why, even though we are able to stay connected to people all over the world, we are lonelier than ever.

How often have you chosen an evening of television or scrolling Facebook over talking to your partner or meeting up with a friend? Even when we are spending real, one-on-one time with Friend A, we tend to be distracted by the social media posts or messages of Friend B. And likewise, when we are with Friend B, we are distracted by the social media posts of Friend A. Snacking on social junk food is tricky in three ways:

» It fulfils our need for connection without giving us real social engagement.

» Because we feel 'full' in the short term, we don't pursue real social interaction.

» Because social junk food makes us feel lonely, we are driven to use social media more and more to feel connected.

These are the ingredients for any addiction, whether it is an addiction to drugs, alcohol, food, shopping, sex or work. They mimic and replace something that is 'the real deal', making us feel 'full' while we are starving at the same time.

Routine

Animals are drawn to routine. To figure out the world around them, they look for cues to understand what will happen next. I remember our family dog going crazy as soon as someone picked up his leash because he quickly learned that this meant going out for a walk. Animals are programmed to look for the consistencies in what is happening around them to help them predict what will happen next so they don't have to stay on high alert all the time. 'Routine' is another word for the habits that allow the brain to calm down so energy can be spent on other things.

Our brain works the same way — routine or predictability can be boring but it reduces stress, calms the system and frees up energy for other things. This is very evident in children. For example, we had a live-in au pair for a few months. When it was time for her to go back home to Germany, my three-and-a-half year old son started wetting his pants again, something he had stopped doing months previously. Processing the change from our au pair being in our home, available to play with him whenever he wanted, to all of a sudden her not being there was a massive change in routine. His little brain needed a lot of energy to process this and, as a result, he regressed in some newly acquired skills. Similarly, when we went away for a weekend with our then ten-month-old baby Isha, the change in routine resulted in her going from just sleeping through the night to waking up at least two or three times per night for two weeks in a row. The change in routine and a new place with other people, as well as sleeping in a different bed, was so much for her brain to process that there wasn't enough energy left to also keep the newly acquired routine of sleeping through the night on track. This doesn't mean that you should never change routines or do fun things that break the routine, but it is good to understand that change requires a lot from a child's brain and temporarily regressing in other areas is a normal consequence. Knowing this can save you a lot of frustration and irritation.

Researchers studied the stress levels in rats given electric shocks. Yes, it's a horrible experiment I know, but the findings are very interesting. The researchers found that the levels of stress present in the rats were not only linked to how strong the shocks were, but also to how predictable they were. The more predictable the shocks, the lower the rats' overall stress levels. The reason for this is that when their brain could predict when the shock was coming, it also knew it could relax in between the shocks. Therefore, overall stress was lowered and burnout was prevented.

When it comes to leading, whether you are leading a family, a small business or a large multinational company, the learning from this is that if your rules, boundaries and consequences are clear and consistent, you are helping the people you lead to thrive by not wasting their energy on unpredictable boundaries and consequences. It creates emotional safety and wellbeing.

It doesn't matter where your boundaries are (within reason of course) as long as they are consistent. If, as a parent, you allow a certain behaviour one day, give three warnings before you intervene the next day, and no warning the day after that, your child's brain will be wasting energy on figuring out where the boundaries are — energy that could be used for learning, playing and fighting viruses.

Every time I look back on a day when I have found myself frustrated with my son, I always come to the same conclusion: I haven't been consistent and, as a result, he starts misbehaving. What really happens is that he is 'looking for the boundaries' and he can't find them because I'm not setting them consistently. When the boundaries depend on my mood or energy levels, I am creating stress in both my brain and that of my children's. Consistent and clear boundaries are, after unconditional love and acceptance, the best possible gift you can give to your children.

Decision fatigue

In adults, a lack of routine is best described as a phenomenon called 'decision fatigue'. A lack of clearly defined 'rules and routines' leads to having to make many decisions. Do I get up at 6 or 7 a.m.? Do I have bread, cereal or muesli for breakfast? Do I have one or two cups of coffee? Do I get dressed before breakfast (and risk getting my child's yoghurt on my work clothes) or after? Do I see four, five or six clients per day? What do I make for dinner? Shall I have a glass of wine or not? Decisions, decisions, decisions — all taking up precious brain energy that could be used for productivity.

Decision fatigue has been studied scientifically and the findings are fascinating. At the beginning of the day, after a good night's sleep, we have plenty of brain energy and, as a result, we make good decisions. But every decision uses up brain power. The later it is in the day, and the more decisions that have been made, the more brain power has been used. Less brain energy is left to make the decisions and then an interesting thing happens — as brain energy is running low, decisions are no longer based on factual logic and reason but instead the brain takes shortcuts to conserve energy and, as a consequence, poor decision-making is likely to occur.

This phenomenon was studied among parole board judges and the researchers found that the likelihood of being granted parole did not depend on the crime, the prison sentence or the ethnic background of the inmate, but rather on the time of day of the hearing. The later in the day the hearing, the less likely it is that you will be given parole. Prisoners who appeared early in the morning received parole about 70 per cent of the time, while those who appeared late in the day were paroled less than 10 per cent of the time. At the beginning of the day the judges had plenty of brain energy to make decisions based on facts and reason, but as the day went on and their brain power began to run low, they became more and more likely to go for the safe shortcut of denying parole.

It wasn't that these judges weren't capable of making good, reasonable decisions, but rather that the mental work of ruling on case after case wore them down. The same principle applies to quarterbacks being prone to dubious choices towards the end of the game, or anyone being able to stick to a diet until 4 p.m. in the afternoon when they cave in and eat all the cookies in the jar.

The more decisions you make in a day, the lower mental energy you will have. Decision fatigue can warp anyone's judgment and the danger is that it mostly happens when you are completely unaware. When energy runs out the brain has two tactics: to go for instant satisfaction by letting willpower off the hook (eat that cookie, buy that dress, or jump on Facebook); or to do nothing and avoid making any decisions. This is why sweets are at the checkout section in the supermarket. After the tiring process of decision-making as you are filling your shopping cart, by the time you are waiting in the queue and the sweets are staring at you, they become hard to resist.

A lack of routine equals an energy leak in your system. You can combat this by structuring your day to avoid making important decisions at the end of it. Creating healthy habits and routines and sticking to them for the most part will leave you with more energy for stress-free productivity.

~

The best decision makers are the ones
who know when not to trust themselves.

— *Roy F Baumeister*

~

Play

The need for play is in our DNA, not just as children but as adults too. You might not consider yourself to be the playful kind, but play and laughter recharges our system like nothing else. Playing is often associated with children and seen as unproductive, but that is far from the truth. Indirectly, play is highly productive and extremely healthy for our body and our mind, plus it's completely free!

There is an abundance of scientific evidence that shows play is fundamental in supporting a whole range of intellectual, emotional and social abilities in children and subsequently in adults. Research on rats showed that playful rats have significantly higher levels of brain-derived neurotrophic factor (BDNF), an important protein that plays a central role in neural plasticity (the flexibility of the brain). Play makes the brain more plastic, thus allowing our learning abilities to increase. Rats that were deprived of play became more aggressive, less social and showed heightened levels of fear and stress.

The function of play is often misunderstood. There is a growing tendency to reduce playtime both at school and at home in order to increase time for learning. This comes from two unfounded beliefs:

» The sooner we start to educate, the better the outcomes will be.

» The more time spent on learning, the better the outcomes will be.

This couldn't be further from the truth. When a child is playing they are learning. Through play, essential cognitive, social and emotional skills are practised, strengthened and established. In addition, play boosts brain plasticity so the brain becomes better and better at learning. When it is time to learn the academic stuff, the brain will be quicker to absorb, understand and use the learned knowledge and skills. In Finland, children don't start school until they are seven years old and school days last no longer than five hours. Even at school there is a strong emphasis on playing and children are given no more than 30 minutes of homework per day. And the PISA (Programme for International Student Assessment) scores that indicate their educational levels and academic outcomes are among the highest in the world.

~

Play is learning and it trains the brain
to become better at learning.

~

As adults we fall into the same unhelpful belief system of thinking that the more we work the better the outcome will be and that playing or having fun isn't productive. We exhaust ourselves mentally throughout the day by not taking breaks and not having fun. As a result, we crash on the couch every evening, tired and drained, and all we have energy left for is to watch TV or browse the Internet.

If we spend some time playing throughout the day, we are recharging our brain power, which will benefit us when we get back to work, leading to higher productivity and better quality of work. This is why every workplace should have table tennis tournaments or something of that nature.

There were once two men who went into the woods to chop down trees. After two hours of work one of the men sits down. He takes a break and sharpens his axe. The other man keeps going, saying, 'I don't have time to take a break. I want to get as much done as possible.' Around lunchtime the first man sits down again, eats his lunch and takes some time to relax and sharpen his axe again. He says to the other man, 'Come on, have some lunch,' but the other man says, 'No, I just don't have the time. I need to keep going.' A couple of hours later the first man sits down again to take another break and sharpens his axe, inviting the other man to take a break but he refuses. At the end of the day, which man has chopped down more trees? It is the first man, who took the breaks, because in the process he sharpened his axe. The other man wore himself out unnecessarily because he didn't take the time to sharpen his axe.

The axe in this story is your brain. Every time you take five minutes to relax and have fun, you are sharpening and recharging your brain. This will prevent you from running out of energy.

When we 'take time out' to play or even to rest, we are not actually pausing our productivity. Our brain is highly productive in the background, sorting information, making links and creating new ideas. Have you ever noticed that the best ideas pop up not when you are working hard but when you are in the shower, walking the dog, driving to work or making a cup of tea?

When you learn to trust your brain, to trust that it naturally works for you and not against you, then you can stop acting like a slave driver to yourself. Have fun, take breaks and as a result you will be even more productive, creative and innovative than before.

〜

Every five minutes of fun will win you
50 minutes of time. Take five, win 50.

〜

As a person, I naturally tend to be more serious than funny and playful. I don't joke around or pull pranks and it takes a lot to make me laugh out loud. It is really thanks to my kids that I have rediscovered the power of playing. My children are too young to understand a deep conversation so we mostly connect through playing and cuddling. And, to be honest, I sometimes find the playing part challenging and very boring. Playing peekaboo and racing with toy cars just isn't my idea of having a good time. But because I care and this is their way to connect and have fun with me, I do it. Not surprisingly though, when I am too busy I tend to postpone the playtime.

When I am in the green brain, the everyday activities become playful. We sing and dance as we tidy up the kitchen together and I don't mind that it takes an extra couple of minutes. And the truth is that when I just do it, when we just go on the trampoline and jump as high as we can, I love it. When I put my baby on my back and together we chase Sem as we pretend to be monsters that are going to eat him, I love it. I love the way they engage in it and laugh, I love the connection, I love the shift in dynamic it creates and I love the feeling of the endorphins it releases in my brain.

As adults, we might need a bit of help creating some regular playtime. Spending time with children and pets can be of great assistance but also playing a sport, board games or just sprinkling some water or soap bubbles in your partner's face can do the trick. Opportunities for play are everywhere; we just need to realize that play is one of the fundamental elements of a happy, fulfilled and productive life.

Our brain and the rest of our body work amazingly well when we give them the fuel they need. When we don't give our body the fuel it needs, we can still be productive but we will have to work harder to achieve the same outcomes, and stress becomes inevitable.

In order to function to the best of our ability, we need all the elements that plants and mammals need. We need real food, clean water and plenty of sun. We need fresh air, enough good-quality sleep and movement. We also need a couple of good relationships, routines that work for us, and plenty of time to play and have fun. Without these elements we can survive but we can't thrive. The good news is that you don't have to perfect all of these in order to have a great working system. Your brain and the rest of your body are flexible and resilient. It isn't until you begin to fall short in many of these areas that your energy levels suffer. However, you can improve your energy levels by making small changes. For example:

» Drink two extra glasses of water a day.

» Go outside for some fresh air and sunshine during your lunchbreak.

» Take the stairs instead of the elevator.

» Order a healthy smoothie instead of that piece of cake.

» Go to bed fifteen minutes earlier.

» Prioritize catching up with your good friends.

» Remember the power of routines and try to stick with the ones that work for you.

» Make time for play, have fun and laugh.

Usually it is more effective to start with small changes. Making changes that are simple will make it more likely that you will keep at it. Over time, small changes can lead to big results.

INSIGHT QUESTIONS: ENERGY

1. Do you have great energy or do you feel tired and drained at the end of the day?

   _____

   _____

   _____

2. If you want to improve your energy levels, take a mindful look at the list below and tick the areas that are in need of some attention:

   ☐ real food

   ☐ clean water

   ☐ plenty of sun

   ☐ fresh air

   ☐ sleep

   ☐ exercise

   ☐ relationships

   ☐ routine

   ☐ play

3. Write down three small steps that you can take to improve energy production in those areas.

   1. _____

      _____

   2. _____

      _____

   3. _____

      _____

INGREDIENT 5:

Passion

*I think it's beautiful the way you sparkle when
you talk about the things you love.*

— *Atticus*

Passion can be defined as an 'uncontrollable emotion associated with passionate love and intense highs and lows'. My personal definition of passion is different. For me, passion is closely related to purpose. It is being drawn to something or someone with undeniable force and comes with a level of doubt and insecurity, but underneath there is a sense of peace — something that feels meant to be.

People's sense of purpose often naturally flows from their passion. They turn what they are passionate about into a goal, a mission they believe in. They set out to achieve something they are passionate about and that becomes their purpose. Having a purpose has the ability to change your sense of identity. It can quite literally give you a *raison d'être*: a reason for existing.

The need for passion and a purpose-driven life is wired deeply into our DNA. It is associated with a sense of happiness that is much deeper than the fleeting happiness that comes from buying new shoes. Deep down we all want to make a difference and add something to the world around us — to have a purpose.

~

The things you are passionate about
are not random, they are your calling.

— *Fabienne Fredrickson*

~

Purpose

When we perceive the way we spend most of our time as meaningless, it zaps the life and motivation out of us and makes life feel like a pointless exercise. But when you find your passion, it is like you are unlocking a hidden storage of super powers. Seeing someone talk about their passion is beautiful. It lights up their face — you can see it in their eyes. It literally makes them shine. And experiencing passion yourself is even better. It gives such energy, excitement and drive that it enables you to move mountains and to do the things you thought were impossible. Tapping into this well of energy is like tapping into a different universe.

Research shows that having a purpose — something you believe to be of importance — is as beneficial for wellbeing as exercising or eating nourishing food. Having a purpose creates healthy, resilient brains that are less likely to suffer from depression and anxiety and have a 50 per cent lower chance of developing Alzheimer's disease. In fact, research shows that the greater the sense of purpose a person has, the lower their risk of developing Alzheimer's is. A seven-year-long study that followed 951 participants showed that having a purpose is also associated with increased levels of happiness, satisfaction and personal growth. It was also linked to greater self-acceptance and better sleep.

Apart from having a beneficial effect on brain health, having a sense of purpose also protects the heart. It has been linked to a 50 per cent reduced risk of stroke or heart attack. These findings point to the stress theory. A lack of purpose in life is linked to higher levels of stress and a different view on stress. People without a clear sense of purpose are likely to deem stress as more problematic and uncomfortable, whereas people with a clear purpose are more likely to interpret stress as a temporary side-effect in the plan of working towards the greater good. This is important because the way you interpret stress affects the potentially damaging effects it has on your system. Research shows that when stress is perceived as bad or harmful, it has a negative impact on the system.

One of my clients is a man in his early fifties. He has worked hard his entire life and created enough financial security two years ago that he could quit his job and retire early. For most this would sound like a dream come true, but this man's happiness went downhill rather than uphill. He fell into a depression. The timing and the nature of the depression indicated that the cause was the fact that he no longer had a purpose. He had no daily duties and no responsibilities — he wasn't needed anywhere. His life felt empty and pointless and all the money in the world couldn't change that. Living a life of just enjoying the fruits of your work isn't as fulfilling and blissful as most people imagine it to be. It made him realize that a large part of his happiness came from his former employment and the interactions that came with it. When he identified the link between his depressive feelings and his retirement, he started a journey of soul searching and asked himself, 'What do I want this phase of my life to be about?' He decided that he would pick up his old profession of photography again but this time he would focus on creative and artistic photography rather than commercial work.

As humans, we crave to have a purpose. We crave the satisfaction of working on things and accomplishing them.

I believe this is, in part, why so many people who have made it financially become active in charities. Sure there will be noble motives involved, but I believe that a large part of their perhaps subconscious motivation is the need to have a purpose. The desire to do more than just play golf or bridge and read the newspaper. It makes us feel good when we have a purpose that goes beyond ourselves and gives back to the community around us. Living a life with purpose and passion comes with a very special mix of chemicals that are released in the brain creating a unique type of happiness and fulfilment. Passion-filled purpose is your green brain on steroids.

~

You have this one life;
what do you want to do with it?

~

Finding your passion

So, finding and doing things you are passionate about makes you healthier and happier. But how do you find your passions? Finding your passions isn't as easy as Hollywood makes it out to be. It is a journey that is constantly jeopardized by the business of life and other roadblocks.

The first thing it's important to realize is that your passion doesn't have to be just one thing. You can have more than one passion and often people will have passions in different areas of life. Your passions can change with time and not every passion has to develop into a life purpose. Passions can be hobbies, interests or vocations. They can be part of everyday life or they can be sitting somewhere on a 'to-do list' collecting dust for many years.

The first step to living a life of passion is identifying what you are passionate about. For some people answering this question is easy, for others it's not. Either way, writing down what you are passionate about will help in creating a life of passion and purpose.

The following Insight Questions will help you to identify what your passions are. Answer them mindfully. Don't judge your answers but allow yourself to write down anything that comes to mind, even if it sounds crazy.

Then mindfully look at your answers and see if you can identify a pattern or a theme. The purpose is to discover what you are passionate about.

INSIGHT QUESTIONS: FIND YOUR PASSION

1. What interests fascinate you?

_____

_____

_____

_____

_____

_____

_____

_____

_____

_____

_____

2. What activities make you feel fully alive?

_____

_____

_____

_____

_____

_____

_____

_____

_____

_____

_____

3. What do you do when you are procrastinating?
    (Facebook and YouTube don't qualify as passions but addictions.)

    _____

    _____

    _____

    _____

    _____

    _____

    _____

    _____

    _____

4. What really, really annoys you?

    _____

    _____

    _____

    _____

    _____

    _____

    _____

    _____

    _____

    _____

    _____

    _____

    _____

5. What would you do for free that others probably wouldn't?

6. What would you do if you knew you only had three years to live?

7. What would you do if you had all the money in the world?

Keeping the first love alive

Just as with any skill or relationship, if you don't make time for it and nourish it, the passion will begin to fade.

One of my clients was struggling with anxiety and depression and when I asked him about his passions in life the first thing that came to mind for him was mountain biking. As he was talking about how much he loves mountain biking, his eyes lit up and his face changed. Where there was heaviness and confusion before, just talking about mountain biking created a lightness and a new perspective. When I asked him when was the last time he went mountain biking, it had been more than six months ago. When I asked him how he could go about getting back into it many obstacles popped up — time, money, distance, feeling too tired, not having anyone to go with. Just as quickly as the sparkle in his eyes had appeared, it disappeared again.

Life is busy and often we don't prioritize the things we are passionate about. We neglect them and then wonder why we feel like our lives don't have meaning and why we feel down. I believe we all have passions and things that make us feel fully alive but prioritizing them, making time for them, is not something all of us do. Just finding out what you are passionate about isn't enough. You need to keep the passion alive by investing time, energy and sometimes money into your passions. It isn't always easy. It isn't always practical. But if you want to optimize your health, energy levels and happiness it's essential.

My husband's passion is cooking. He is at his happiest when he can spend hours in the kitchen preparing an Italian meal from scratch. Yet I used to do most of the cooking because it was more practical for me to cook most days. Even though I love eating good food, cooking dinner isn't really my idea of fun. When we were talking about our passions and how we can make more time for them, we realized that he loves cooking while I dislike it, yet I do most of the cooking. It just didn't make sense. The practicalities were an obstacle but with some creative thinking and changing our schedule, we reorganized our lives in a way that allows Pieter to do most of the cooking and we are all happier as a result.

INSIGHT QUESTION: NEGLECTED PASSIONS

1. Have you neglected your passions?

   _____

   _____

2. If the answer is 'Yes' then ask yourself, 'How can I prioritize them again? What small step can I take to start spending time on my passions again?' Then mindfully write down anything that comes to mind.

   _____

   _____

   _____

   _____

   _____

   _____

   _____

   _____

   _____

   _____

   _____

   _____

   _____

   _____

   _____

   _____

~

Create a life that you don't
want to take a vacation from.

~

Instead of trying to make room in your busy life for your passions, you can also turn it around. You can build a life around you that you are passionate about. I know it isn't always possible and it is almost never easy. I myself once thought that it simply wasn't possible for me but by taking small steps (some full of fear) I made it happen and found out it wasn't impossible after all.

Building your life around your passions sometimes means changing careers, but sometimes it means being creative about your current job and adding or focusing more on the elements you are passionate about.

Another client of mine is an artistic, contemplative person who loves people and nature. Her passion is pottery. When she is creating ceramics she feels like she is in heaven. She works in an art gallery, but since a change in management, her works consists of more than 40 hours a week of paperwork. She came to me for depressive symptoms. She felt exhausted, drained, down and lacked self-confidence. When we came to the topic of work she explained that most of her days were spent in a back room of the gallery with no windows, behind a computer, doing organizational things that have very little to do with arts or people. It came as a shock when I told her that no amount of mindfulness would make her happy in a job that doesn't suit her personality and passions. We started trying to add in elements that she is passionate about to her work — moving her desk to the gallery itself where she would interact more with people, volunteering for projects that have more creativity in them and eating lunch in the gallery garden every day. These changes helped a little but not enough, and even though it wasn't easy for her to leave her job, she did. She found a job managing a pottery workshop and a pottery shop in a small beach community and her depression vanished.

The blocks to living a passion-filled life include many factors, such as time, energy, money, work identity and personal insecurities.

Time

In 1964, writer Isaac Asimov predicted that by 2014 the biggest problem of humanity would be boredom. He argued that since machines will have taken over most of the work, we would have too much time on our hands and as a result we would suffer from boredom. Asimov was right about machines taking over most of the work. We don't have to do laundry by hand or kill and pluck the chicken we eat. Many household chores and jobs have been taken over by technology. He was wrong, however, about humans having too much time on their hands. We are more time poor than ever. In the supermarket we look for the shortest queue and become annoyed when it turns out we didn't pick the fastest one. Getting stuck in traffic feels like a big deal. Losing only a couple of minutes can annoy the hell out of us. Work hours have increased drastically for most families. The norm used to be having one of the adult family members working full time; now it is having two adults working full time just to be able to pay the bills (in most countries at least). We have more technology but less time for ourselves and for our passions. Stress has become normal. Taking time to do what you love has become a luxury and something that can make us feel guilty.

Asimov also predicted that by 2014 entertainment would play a huge role in our lives and a result of this entertainment overload would be a drastic increase in mental health problems. He was right about that too. Entertainment is everywhere and, like Asimov predicted, it has become so ingrained into our lives that it's almost impossible to escape it. I think our ancestors would roll over in their graves if they knew we spend almost every minute of our free time watching a screen.

There is nothing wrong with technology nor with entertainment, but when it leaves hardly any room for doing the things we are passionate about, we are missing out on valuable green-brain-inducing activities. After an evening of watching TV, watching YouTube clips or reading blogs, no one has ever said, 'Well that was an evening well spent. I feel so fulfilled.'

~

You don't have time, you make time.

~

I remember thinking to myself, 'I just don't have the time to do the things I love. My life is too busy', until I did a little experiment. For one week I started clocking how much time I spent on social media, watching TV or other random videos and blogs. When I saw how much time I actually spent on this, I became painfully aware that my excuse was nonsense. I had many hours a week to do the things I am passionate about. The problem wasn't a lack of time but how I spent my time.

Energy

Pursuing the activities and interests we are passionate about gives us energy, but before they refuel and refill us, we need to put in energy to make it happen. Doing things you are passionate about might take planning and organizing. You actually need to drag yourself to the gym, show up for that Italian class, read those books, or go out to the shops to buy the art supplies. It costs less energy to sit down on the sofa, turn on the TV and flick from one program to the next. It costs less energy to watch videos about what you love than to actually do what you love. When our systems are low on energy, it becomes very hard to find the energy and motivation to do the things that you know will make you feel better. Mustering up the self-discipline to get back into doing the things you love can feel impossible when your energy is low at the end of the day. But with passions there are simply no shortcuts; you only get the benefits if you muster up the energy to actually do them and keep doing them. It is like a relationship: if you don't invest in it, it will slowly die.

One of my clients is a police officer who has a busy job and a family with young children. His passion is surfing but the business of life makes it really challenging for him to fit surfing in. When he isn't working he is spending time with his family and surfing is put on the backburner. Yet surfing is the one thing that makes him feel totally at peace. It calms his mind and puts him in what we call the 'state of flow'. In the state of flow, what we do feels effortless and the world around us stands still. For him, when he is surfing, all that exists is him and the waves. After a morning or afternoon of surfing he feels refreshed and full of energy. Things that felt like a big deal before he hit the water don't feel overwhelming anymore when he leaves the water. He comes to see me every now and then as his symptoms of anxiety resurface and one of the first things I always ask him is, 'When did you last go surfing?'

The things that we are passionate about are not luxuries. They are essential to our mental health and happiness. Plus they are more fun and cheaper than seeing a psychologist.

Money

Another block that often stops us from building a life around our passions is money. A job that embodies what we are passionate about won't always be the best paying job. We often do jobs we don't like just to pay the bills and it can be scary giving up financial stability.

Sacrificing financial security isn't something to take lightly, but it also doesn't have to be something to rule out. Like anything, money is a concept and so is the belief that we need a certain amount of money to get by. The problem is that we often look at our current situation, our current expenses and our current bank statement and decide what we can and cannot afford based on these factors. When we use this approach we don't notice that our expenses tend to grow at the same speed as our income and, as a result, no matter where we are at, we will never be able to 'afford' a big life change or a career change.

Just a few years ago I was stuck in a job that I hated. It was a reputable and well-paying job and my husband and I had just arrived in New Zealand. I was the main breadwinner at that time because my husband was still looking for work. This job seemed like a great opportunity but in reality it was horrible. It sucked the life out of me and every day I dreaded going to work. I spent most of my time writing long and detailed psychological reports that would end up collecting dust in a large cabinet filled with more of the same reports. The whole thing felt so pointless and frustrating that it was hard to bear. One thing that would get me through the day and stopped me from walking out the door was that I calculated what I made per day and what I needed to pay the bills. According to my calculations I needed to stay. I couldn't afford to quit or we would lose our house.

I clearly remember one day after work when we were at the gym. I had just had another day at work filled with frustration and I said to Pieter, 'I just can't take it anymore. I would rather lose our house and live in a campervan than work there one more day of my life.' And I meant it, I really did. My frustration had grown bigger than my fear of being without a job and homeless. It was in that moment that my definition of what I could 'afford' drastically changed. It changed from 'I need to be able to afford to pay the rent' to 'I can't afford to stay in this job one more day'. I would rather be poor and free to spend my days doing something that makes me happy than be 'rich' and miserable. When that shift happened, all of a sudden the idea of living in a campervan changed from horrible, poor, shameful and going nowhere to kind of exciting, a new adventure and a possibility to be financially free and independent. My biggest fear of becoming homeless all of a sudden felt more like going on a long holiday. The next day I handed in my resignation.

~

It's better to be poor and happy
than to be financially secure and miserable.

~

What we can and cannot afford is a concept that will be a reality as long as we believe in it. The truth is that if we are willing to give up our current lifestyle and the luxuries that we have grown accustomed to, we can afford almost anything. As often happens in life, as soon as I made the leap of faith, trusting that it would work out one way or another, Pieter found a job within a week. We didn't have to live in a campervan after all, but the mental freedom from thinking we needed a stable income has stayed with me and has been invaluable.

Last year I was saw two clients on the same day. The first client was a psychology student who was suffering from depression and chronic fatigue. She had a part-time cleaning job, which made it possible for her to see me. She felt that she needed to do something about her mental health; for her, it simply wasn't an option not to get help. Later that same day I saw a woman who is a general manager in a large corporation.

She was coming to see me because she was struggling with anxiety and marital problems. She worked hard, was well-off and was living what seemed to me a luxurious lifestyle. She cancelled her second appointment because her husband lost his contract and she felt she couldn't afford to see me anymore.

This showed me so clearly that the amount of money we think we need is just a concept. What we think we can afford is just a belief. The student who saw me weekly for about a year cleaned houses three hours a week to be able to see me. She felt she could afford it and she made it work. The general manager of the large corporation, who I am sure would have had much more money than the student, felt that she couldn't afford it.

A few years after I had quit the job in which I wasn't happy, Pieter found himself at a similar point in life. By then I had started my psychology practice and we had started a family. Our oldest child was three at the time and our second child was on the way. We had chosen to not have our children in full-time day care so, as a result, I was being a mum during the day and seeing clients in the evening and weekends. I loved my new job and the practice grew and grew. Pieter, who was working more than 60 hours a week as a finance manager, hated his job and came home every day grumpy and frustrated. I must admit that I probably wasn't the most supportive and patient partner. After you have made the jump yourself and you have experienced how freeing and rewarding it is, it can be hard to bear the daily complaining of someone who is still in a job they are unhappy with. I often told him to just quit his job and that we would be fine, we would find a way to make it work, but he would always reply, 'We can't afford it.'

Pieter, being an accountant and feeling responsible for paying the bills and providing for his family, didn't quite see the light yet. He felt the heat though when I finally gave him an ultimatum. After a long and emotional talk about how I had had it working two jobs (being a stay-at-home mum during the day and working in the evenings and weekends) and his long work hours in a job he didn't like and then having to deal with his bad moods as a result, I said to him, 'Either you quit your job, or I quit my job, or our kids start their full-time day care career.' The best choice was obvious. I loved my job, he hated his job and we both didn't want our children to go into full-time day care. The only thing that kept him there was financial security. It was the scariest decision of his life but he decided to quit.

It took some time for him to experience the freedom I had experienced after making the decision to start a new job. It turned out that it wasn't only losing the financial security that made the transition hard for him; his job was a large part of his identity.

Work identity

Our job can give us a sense of identity, a sense of belonging and being useful in the world. Also, jobs can provide a sense of pride and prestige. In the movie *The Devil Wears Prada* we get a perfect glimpse of why some people choose to work crazy hours for little or no pay and put up with horrendous treatment from their seniors just to be able to add a big name to their CV. It seems crazy yet some do this voluntarily and happily. The same phenomenon can be seen in any sector, from finance to healthcare. We are drawn to 'big names' in our industry because being associated with a big name gives prestige. Any job can make us feel important and needed and that is a nice feeling. Your job can become a large part of who you are and how you see yourself. This is why when people are asked to describe themselves, in the western world at least, their job title often comes right after their name. When Pieter quit his job he struggled with the questions 'Who am I?' 'How am I contributing to society?' The fact that he wasn't lounging around all day but was actually looking after our children and taking care of the household kept him busy, but it didn't feel to him like he was doing anything useful. Comments from friends and even strangers he would meet when he was out with the kids didn't help. They would ask questions like, 'Do you have a day off?' and 'Are you in between jobs?'

Our society views it as more respectable to work more than 60 hours a week than have a great work–life balance. Hardly seeing your children and bordering on burnout gives you a badge of honour, while raising your own children and enjoying Monday mornings at the beach makes people think you are lazy. As Ricardo Semler put it, 'We have learned how to work on Sunday nights, but we haven't learned to go to the movies on Tuesday afternoon.'

Stepping out of the box of what is considered 'normal' by the people around you is scary. People around you probably won't understand and in a way you will need to redefine who you are.

You don't always need to make big life changes to make more room for your passions. Sometimes it is a matter of redesigning your current job or re-evaluating how you spend your free time.

One of my clients comes from a family of pilots and she also works as a pilot. She has studied for years to become a pilot and has worked hard to master the required skills. However, she doesn't love it; she actually has a fear of flying. What she loves and spends most of her free time doing is lifting weights. She has an amazing dedication and when she sets a goal she will do anything it takes to accomplish it. With her natural determination she has trained her brain to beat depression, conquered an eating disorder, built a brand new life all on her own on the other side of the world and has worked up the courage to leave a relationship that wasn't working. This woman basically has the words 'personal trainer' written on her forehead. But she is a pilot and studied many years to become one and she has to pay her bills. Sometimes I wish I could just say to her, 'Who cares? To hell with your degree and your fancy job. Follow your heart!' but life often isn't that simple. So we look for the 'wriggle room' — ways we can shape her job into something that suits her better and has more of what she is passionate about. In her case, that is becoming an instructor for pilots in training.

INSIGHT QUESTIONS: YOUR JOB

1. What do you love about your current job?

    _____

    _____

    _____

2. What do you dislike about your current job?

    _____

    _____

    _____

3. Can you think of ways you could do more of what you like?

    _____

    _____

    _____

    _____

    _____

4. Can you think of ways to delegate or do less of what you dislike?

    _____

    _____

    _____

    _____

    _____

Insecurities

Passions that go beyond hobbies sometimes demand risk-taking. They can go hand in hand with insecurities. Stepping out and living your passion is a powerful process. It can be something that upsets the balance and messes with the securities and predictabilities we have created and built into our lives — and our brain objects to this. Our brain is risk averse and living life to the fullest is risky business. Being fully alive often means letting go of the very things that keep us comfortable and secure. It means moving out of the box into the unknown, into a place we are not sure about and where we question whether we have got what it takes to succeed. It's a stretch, which is the very nature of a passionate and purpose-filled life because without stretching there is no trusting and no growing.

The only thing I can say is, 'Just do it'. Go on, just do it. It might be scary, it might seem crazy, it might feel impossible and there might be no one to support you or encourage you, but just do it anyway. You may never feel ready, it may never be the right time, but it's better to be poor and happy than to have money and be miserable. Courage isn't the absence of fear; it is doing the right thing with trembling knees.

~

*If you can keep your eye fixed on the purpose,
you can keep the passion alive and do things
you thought were impossible.*

~

As I am writing this, I am on the brink of another big life change — moving from the city to the country. The following steps illustrate the way I reached my passion:

1. **Identifying your passion:** Life hints at what it is I really want. Every time we are in a rural place I feel so good and I can't help but fantasize about how amazing life would be living on a farm. I can see myself waking up, stepping outside, looking at a majestic view, breathing in the fresh air, looking at the animals and feeling refreshed, alive and grateful. Then my fantasy fast-forwards to seeing my kids run around in bare feet with the lambs we will have and then to dinners with friends at a long wooden table underneath a big oak tree. It isn't just fun, it's fun with a layer of belonging and peace. There is a still and deep voice that tells me THIS is what I really want.

2. **Focusing on your passion:** Then life goes on as usual and I don't think about this dream until a situation, an event or someone creates momentum, and all of a sudden I get a glimpse of the possibility of this fantasy actually becoming a reality.

3. **Fighting the obstacles:** That is when the panic monster shows up and ruins the momentum with its beautiful music in the background by scratching the record and starting the worry theme song. My panic monster has four secret weapons:

    a. You can't afford it.

    b. You will regret it.

    c. There will be no way back.

    d. What will people think?

I have battled the panic monster many times in my life but he keeps getting under my skin and makes me wonder *why*. Why do I want this? What was I thinking? It's too hard. It's too complicated. I don't have what it takes. What will people think? Then there are two options: to give up or to persevere.

4. **Overcome the obstacles and make it happen:** I tap into the purpose-filled passion that unlocks courage, energy and motivation to do what I deemed impossible. (Either that or I talk my husband into selling the house so there is no way back and I desperately hope to discover that once we have moved it will all work out for the best!)

INGREDIENT 6:

Perseverance

~

*The man on top of the mountain
didn't fall there.*

— *Vince Lombardi*

~

After you have identified what you are passionate about, there are two options: will it stay a dream forever or will you make it a reality? For the most part the outcome will depend on your ability to keep the passion alive, to make it enduring and to keep going when the going gets tough. This is largely determined by your level of perseverance or grit — the next ingredient needed for stress-free productivity.

If we insert grit into the car analogy it becomes this: for stress-free productivity that leads to successfully achieving your goals (your destination), you first of all need to turn on the engine and put it in the right gear. This represents switching on your green brain on a daily basis. You need to have plenty of good-quality petrol in your car to fuel the engine. The petrol represents food, water, fresh air, sunshine, exercise and sleep — all the things your body needs for fuel so the engine of your body can create great energy to power the drive. Then you need to know where you are going (your goal). This represents having clear goals based on your passion and purpose. The next step is to figure out the directions: where to turn left and where to turn right. This involves avoiding detours so you stay clear of frustrations and unnecessary delays. This represents your focus and goal-orientated decision-making and prioritizing. The next element you need is perseverance to overcome the inevitable obstacles that you will bump into along the way. There are always bumps and obstacles to overcome — success never comes easy.

Intelligence

For a long time researchers have studied what makes people successful; why Person A makes it and Person B doesn't. This area of research has looked at countless attributes with by far most of the focus going on intelligence. Most people believe you have to be smart to be successful. The theory that intelligence equals outcome has shaped much of how we prepare for success. It's all about being smart and educated, or is it?

A recent meta-analysis of the studies analyzing what sets highly successful people apart from others paints a different picture. It shows that intelligence isn't as predictive of success as many people assume.

I always did well in school and graduated with honours. One would assume I must be fairly intelligent but I remember clearly that when I was conducting intelligence tests as part of my work as an intern, I often thought to myself, 'I don't think I will score very high on this.' My spelling is horrible, I'm bad at math, I'm bad at puzzles, I'm bad at quizzes and my memory only works well regarding topics I am interested in. I see the same thing with many young people I test. Their IQ scores are not impressive, but when I ask them about something they are passionate about, I often discover a very bright person.

Just the other day my son was invited to a 'before school check'. This is a standard developmental screening that all four year olds take in New Zealand. The nurse asked him if he could count to ten and he said no (even though he can). Then she asked him to name the circle, square, triangle and rectangle on a piece of paper and he could only name the circle and the square. Then she asked him if he could write his name and he said no. She turned her attention to me and asked if he goes to the toilet by himself. The answer was no. Does he brush his own teeth? The answer was no. Does he dress himself? The answer was again no. Her look became more and more disapproving and she hinted that he was behind in his development because 'a four year old should be able to do all these things'.

She didn't take into consideration that he had turned four just two weeks ago. Nor did she take into consideration that he can play for hours building complicated train tracks, empties the dishwasher, tidies up his toys, understands his emotions and is able to talk about them, understands other people's emotions and responds to them, is able to establish a friendship with a new child in the playground within a minute, and speaks and understands two languages. As parents we care more about his social skills, emotion regulation skills and ability to be a contributing member of our family than we care about him being able to dress himself and write his name. So these are the things we have encouraged and worked on with him. What you focus on grows. Measuring intelligence and development based on a standardized framework will fall short for most people.

You can compare standardized intelligence tests to fishing. When you let down your net and bring it back up, you count how many fish are in it. You count how many fish you have caught. When you then assume that this must be all the fish in the ocean because these are all the fish you have caught, you are making a big error. You have only caught the ones that fit the size of the net and you have only caught the ones that were in the spot where you were fishing.

Intelligence comes in many different forms and standardized tests only capture a fraction of it. Yet a lot of emphasis is put on them, which comes with a risky side-effect: self-fulfilling prophecies. Studies show that if a teacher believes a child is intelligent, the child will perform better. Why? Because of the *expectation* that the child will perform well. This expectation leads to more positive interactions, more support and more opportunities to learn. The expectation that the child will perform well creates an environment that stimulates and enables high performance. If the child performs poorly, the teacher will think they are just having a bad day; if the child performs well, the teacher will think it is a confirmation of the child's intelligence. Unfortunately, believing that a child is unintelligent will also create a self-fulfilling prophecy leading to more negative interactions, less support and fewer opportunities to grow and learn. Mistakes will be viewed as a confirmation of the lack of intelligence, and good performance will be deemed luck or attributed to external factors.

Talent

Another misconception is that success is a result of talent. Research shows that most of us are more attracted to the concept of 'talented people' or 'naturals' than we are to 'hard-working' or 'persevering' individuals. Even among parents there seems to be subtle competition going on about how talented their children are compared to other children. We think children need rewards, recognition and praise to show them (and the parents) how talented and gifted they are. There is nothing worse than being 'average' and every parent seems to think their child is 'high achieving'. Not only does this put enormous pressure on the child, creating a potential breeding ground for anxiety and self-esteem issues later on, it is also a misconception that talent directly leads to being successful and happy in life. As researcher Angela Duckworth puts it, 'We overemphasize talent and underemphasize everything else. This leads to another thinking error; when we think someone is talented we think it is their talent, not their effort that led to their success.'

If intelligence and talent are not the key to success, there must be another important factor in the mix. Having looked at factors such as background, resources and even attractiveness, the researchers found that the one consistent factor shared by successful leaders in every field included in the study was not intelligence or talent, but grit.

Without ongoing effort and without perseverance, talent and intelligence won't lead to excellence. This is an interesting finding because grit isn't talked about much. Many people have never even heard of the concept and its direct link to achievements and success. Angela Duckworth describes grit as a combination of passion and perseverance. Approaching things as a marathon instead of a sprint. Keeping your eye on the long-term goals, day in and day out, without losing focus, and working steadily towards your goals. Not giving up when there is little or no indication of success but sticking to your goals until you have achieved them. Students with grit are more likely to graduate, salespeople with grit are more likely to be top sellers; in every field, people with grit are more likely to be successful.

How do you get grit?

If you want to be gritty it helps to have a passion — a strong interest in something. Why? I think for most of us it would be simply too difficult to be gritty in an area or with a subject we are not passionate about. It would become too boring, too laborious. Without having a passion for it, most of us would sooner or later give up and move on to something else. But just having a passion isn't enough. Passion without determination and perseverance for long-term goals can lead to jumping from one area of interest to another without really mastering skills or achieving outcomes. The combination of passion and perseverance is the key to great outcomes. First identifying what you are passionate about and then dedicating yourself to it by setting short-term and long-term goals and sticking to them, tirelessly working towards them until they have been realized, is the key to realizing your dreams.

Grit also grows when we feel our passion, our goal, serves a greater purpose. If we believe that what we are doing doesn't only benefit us but will also benefit others in a way we think is important or necessary, then grit grows. When you are struggling or experiencing a setback, reminding yourself of the purpose of what you are doing will help you get up and try again.

Sometimes it is my passion that drives me to coach and counsel clients and to write and do public speaking. I love what I do and when everything goes smoothly I find it a lot of fun. But things don't always go to plan. When I hit a roadblock or setback, the passion that was so strong before can suddenly evaporate and it all just feels like hard work for very little benefit. During those times I often feel like giving up and getting a 'normal job', something easy, where I can work and then go home and relax. At those times it is the purpose of my work that helps me to keep going and not throw in the towel. I believe my work is valuable and that it changes people's lives. I believe my material contributes in a significant way. It is easy to forget at times that, through the work I have done, people have overcome traumas, parents have learned to understand and validate their children's emotions, relationships have been restored and marriages have been saved. Those things matter to me — they matter a lot. When I hit a roadblock and can't find my grit, I sometimes make myself read messages that people have sent me about how my work has changed their lives.

Hi Chantal,

I would like to order another book. I have lent mine to my daughter-in-law who is going through a hard and stressful time with work at the moment. The book is helping her so much she now calls it her 'security blanket'. She carries it around in her handbag everywhere she goes and doesn't want to give it back!

Thank you for all that you do.

Kind regards,
Pamela

~

Hi Chantal,

I've just got your latest newsletter and, as ever, I love it. You offer the best 'free stuff' — ways to feel better and be better in this hectic world of ours. The 'three steps' exercise is so valuable — I instantly broke the chains of a bad memory. I got so much out of the workshop you presented (last year? the year before?) with Kathryn Burnett, and I often use the techniques you both taught to spark creativity in my working life. It's crucial — I'm a writer in an agency where quality is key to our reputation, and time is money.

Inez

Hi Chantal,

Your workshop covered the psychological, neuroscience and practical dimensions of mindfulness better than I have ever been exposed to before ... My parents are Buddhists and in the past had tried to teach me meditation (but I was at the age when I was not keen to accept my parents' good intentions!), but also over the last few years my psychological colleagues at work (I'm currently employed as a medical doctor training in psychiatry) have tried to impart some of their knowledge but not with the same breadth as you were able to do in a short period of time ... so congratulations and thanks again!

Mangala — MD in training

When the road is smooth, it is my passion for my work that drives me to grow and learn and keep going. When setbacks happen, it is my purpose-fuelled grit that helps me to persevere.

You don't have to be in a helping profession to have a sense of purpose. Purpose can be found in almost any profession. A beautiful example that I have heard several times and recently came across again in Angela Duckworth's book is this:

~

A bricklayer was asked why he lays bricks.
His response was to pay his bills
— he has a job.

Another bricklayer was asked why he lays bricks.
His response was to build a church
— he has a career.

Another bricklayer was asked why he lays bricks.
His response was he was building the house of God
— he has a calling.

~

Whatever you do can be a job, a career or a calling. It doesn't matter what you do, it is how you see it that matters. According to research, the people who see what they do as their calling, whether it is being a CEO, a cleaner, a teacher or driving a bus, will not only be grittier, they will also be happier, more productive and experience work as more rewarding.

This doesn't only apply to your job. You can literally apply it to anything and change your experience of that activity. One day I was doing grocery shopping and I really don't like grocery shopping. The shop was busy, I was in a rush and I was pretty grumpy because I had to do the weekly shopping. In the middle of the shop I stopped, I noticed my frown and noticed, with kindness, how grumpy I was. Then I chose to be grateful (it's the quickest thing to get me out of a bad mood). In my mind I said, 'I am so grateful and thankful that I can buy all this food to feed my family.' In that moment shopping went from being a chore to caring for my family. I went from buying stuff to buying ingredients that would make healthy meals for our children to grow. I went from buying what was on the list to picking out a nice bottle of wine for my husband and me to enjoy in the evening. All I changed was my perspective and it changed both my experience and my mood.

Changing your perspective on something can change your experience of that thing or activity. This can be applied to any activity, but work (in or outside of the home) is a great starting point.

INSIGHT QUESTIONS
SAMPLE

1. What kind of work do you do? *I'm a librarian.*

2. Why do you do this?
    Self-focused: *To pay my bills.*
    Other-focused: *I help people find the books they are looking for.*
    Values-focused: *Because I believe reading enriches people's lives.*

INSIGHT QUESTIONS: WORK

1. What kind of work do you do?

    _____

    _____

    _____

2. Why do you do this?

    Self-focused: _____

    _____

    _____

    Other-focused: _____

    _____

    _____

    Values-focused: _____

    _____

    _____

3. When you have a setback, how do you usually respond?
    What thoughts, feelings and behaviours are activated?

    _____

    _____

4. When are moments that you experience grit? What thoughts, feelings
    and actions go hand in hand with grit for you? Notice the link and
    practise and strengthen those thoughts and actions.

    _____

    _____

    _____

~

A smooth sea never made a skilled sailor.

~

Research has found a strong link between grit and having a growth mindset. A growth mindset is the belief that your abilities and therefore the outcomes of your efforts are not fixed, but that you are able to learn and grow as a result of effort and consistent practice. A growth mindset comes with the belief that learning includes failing, starting over again and doing a better job the second, third or even fiftieth time around. Keeping your eye on the goal and on your why helps you to not focus on the bumps in the road and let them derail you. It helps you to keep your eyes 'above the waves', focused on the goal.

There is a high school in Chicago where when a student doesn't pass a test they score it with 'not yet'. This embodies the whole concept of a growth mindset. There is a huge difference in hearing that you failed a test or that you haven't passed it *yet*. The first message hints at an inability, the second points to a growing ability. The first message feels like an end point whereas the second message indicates you are on a learning curve and need to do a bit more learning.

The growth mindset sets people up for more and better learning. One way this shows up in the research is during the feedback phase in scientific testing. During one such study children were identified as having either a growth or a fixed mindset. Then they were given challenging tasks to perform and after that they were given their scores. During this process they were hooked onto a device that measures brain activity. Researchers found a distinct difference in the brains of children with a fixed mindset versus children with a growth mindset. As soon as the children with the fixed mindset had learned their scores, the brain activity died down. Their brain went 'offline'. For them, the scores were the end station. They weren't very interested in learning the right answers to the questions they had answered wrongly, which was shown by a significant drop in their brain activity when they were shown the right answers to the questions they got wrong. However, the brain activity of the children with the growth mindset showed the opposite response. Their brains would become highly active when they were told the right answers to the questions they had answered wrong. They were engaged, paying attention, and the high levels of brain activity indicate they were deeply processing the information and learning from the feedback they were receiving.

A growth mindset is about learning and therefore it enhances learning. Research shows that when teachers educate based on the growth-mindset principle, learning and self-esteem in the children increases and, as a result, so do test scores.

Having a growth mindset and being willing to fail go hand in hand. To someone with a growth mindset, failing isn't a definite statement about their abilities and it isn't a reason to stop either. Having a growth mindset doesn't mean you have to enjoy failing but it makes not passing a natural part of the process. Because the scores aren't an indication of ability but rather an indication of where you are on the learning curve, 'failing' isn't as personal or as intrusive for someone with a growth mindset as it is for someone with a fixed mindset. Instead, 'failing' becomes a valuable indicator of what you need to focus your practice on.

Becoming better at persevering and not being negatively affected by failing sounds very appealing for many people, and the great news is that you can attain both grit and a growth mindset. A good place to start is to redefine failure — to stop seeing it as something you want to avoid and begin to see it as a natural and normal part of the process of success. Redefining 'failure' to 'learning' and redefining 'not passing' to 'not yet passing' can be a great way to do this. It might seem like just a change of words but to your brain it will be much more than that.

Just say these sentences out loud and notice the difference in how they make you feel:

I have failed	versus	I haven't succeeded at that yet.
I can't do it	versus	I can't do it yet.
I'm not good at ...	versus	I'm not good at ... yet.

For most people, the first sentences will trigger negative emotions, including insecurity, vulnerability or shame and for most people the second sentences will feel more neutral. The first sentences erode our self-esteem whereas the second sentences are a neutral description of a present reality. Changing the words that you use is a very powerful tool in changing the way you think and feel. To attain a growth mindset I recommend deleting the first sentences from your vocabulary and replacing them with the more helpful ones.

Locus of control

A fixed mindset means that we believe that we are good or bad at something and that we can do nothing or very little to change that. You either have it or you don't and if you don't you might as well give up. A fixed mindset leads to an experienced *external* locus of control, the feeling that the outcome depends on factors we cannot influence. To someone with a fixed mindset, making a mistake is an indication of a lack of talent or ability and it becomes a negative predictor of outcome.

A growth mindset means we have the belief that through consistent and deliberate practice we will grow our skills and abilities. A growth mindset leads to an *internal* locus of control — the belief that the ability to change the situation lies with us, that it depends on what we do rather than what we have been given.

A growth mindset can be incredibly liberating because it helps us see that success comes from what we are willing to put in. Outcomes don't just come from luck, talent, intelligence or money; they also come from practice and perseverance. Of course, all of the above play a role in outcome, but more so because things like intelligence, talent and support influence how fast the growth will happen. The main factor responsible for outcome is the amount of ongoing practice — the effort — you put in. This leads to more positive and helpful thoughts, such as:

» I can do it if I practise enough.
» Nothing is impossible if I dedicate myself to it for long enough.
» I can do it; I just need to figure out how to optimize my practice.

Trust the process

All of this is in line with what we know from neuroscience. Our brains are incredibly plastic and changeable. What we practise literally becomes stronger in our brains. In my first year of studying psychology, I learned a simple example of how changeable the brain is and it truly fascinated me. We were shown an image of the part of the brain that controls the fingertips of the left hand. Then the participants in the study were taught to play the violin and several weeks later the same brain area was captured in a scan. The parts of the brain that are directly linked to the fingertips of the left hand had grown significantly. Through playing the violin daily and using the fingertips of their left hand in a new, deliberate and consistent way, the brain area linked to the fingertips of their left hand grew in size! As they were growing their ability to play the violin they were growing their brain.

This principle applies to everything you can think of that you can practise. You become better at what you practise because your brain rewires itself as a result of it.

However, not all practice is equal. Research shows that the most efficient and effective way to practise is to:

» Set clear and stretching goals.
» Practise with undivided attention and great effort.

» Track your progress, identify your areas of weakness and focus on them deliberately.

Of course, talent and intelligence helps — they will make your learning faster — and having opportunities is important too. If you are dedicated to learning to play the piano but you don't have access to a piano, it becomes impossible to practise. Having great coaches and teachers is a huge benefit too. But more predictive of achievement is consistent effort and ongoing practice, which is within your control.

Sometimes, however, the best way to learn and speed up growth is to make commitments that are impossible to back out of. One example of this comes from one of my former clients, a man who felt burnt out and suicidal. It wasn't that he didn't want to live, but sometimes life was just too much to bear. When I asked him what it was that kept him alive his answer was, 'My children.' As we were talking about strategies, things we could put in place to make sure that during those times of despair he wouldn't take his life but would hold on and remind himself of his children, he came up with something that wasn't only very effective, but was also heartwarming. Whenever he would feel himself go backwards, he would make a promise to one of his children. He would promise one of them that during the weekend he would buy them an ice cream, or he would promise them that on Wednesday afternoon he would take them to the park. He considered himself a man of his word and because he had made them a promise he simply couldn't take his life because it would mean he wouldn't be around to buy them the ice cream or take them to the park. Sometimes making commitments that we practically or emotionally feel we cannot back out of can help us stay on track with what we want to accomplish, even if what we want to accomplish is staying alive.

Sometimes it is your passion that fuels the pursuit of your goals; sometimes it is your perseverance. Without passion, the joy is sucked out of the pursuit; without perseverance, you will give up when the going gets tough. Reaching your goals doesn't come easy; if it does you might want to rethink your goals and challenge yourself a bit more. Great development and achievements come from perseverance and that is part of the beauty of it all. If it came easy it wouldn't be as rewarding. Easy success isn't as much fun as success that took perseverance, because easy success doesn't challenge us and it doesn't build character. There are no shortcuts to real, fulfilling and sustainable success. It is supposed to be a journey filled with challenges.

INSIGHT QUESTIONS: SKILLS

1. What skill do you want to learn or become better at?

    _____

    _____

    _____

    _____

2. Set a clear goal for yourself when it comes to this skill.

    _____

    _____

    _____

    _____

3. What practise routine would work for you? Don't make it too hard to realize, but also not too easy or the lack of achievement will dampen your motivation.

    _____

    _____

    _____

    _____

4. How can you receive regular feedback on your progress? Do you need to get in touch with other people who are doing the same thing? Do you need a coach or to sign up for an online program?

    _____

    _____

    _____

    _____

Enjoyment of the process

~

Trust the process.

~

My very first introduction to mindfulness was during my postgraduate internship over lunch with Dr Annemarie Post, one of the psychologists I was observing and learning the art of psychology from. She said to me, 'You can ride your bike to get to work or you can ride your bike and get to work.' This was a light-bulb moment for me.

What she meant was that you can ride your bike to work each day (in the Netherlands bicycles are the main means of transportation) with the sole purpose of transporting your body from home to the office or you can start the day with an enjoyable bike ride and arrive at the office at the end of it. It might seem like a subtle difference but it was a revelation to me.

Those simple words became a metaphor and a welcome new perspective for the striving perfectionist I was at that time. I was dedicated, focused, eager to learn, motivated to become good at my profession, hard-working and saw the purpose of what I was there to do. All the ingredients for success were there but I was so focused on the goal that I was forgetting to enjoy the process. I was forgetting to pause, look around and take it all in. I was grateful to be given this incredible opportunity to work with these giants in my field, but I was forgetting to enjoy it.

Perfectionism

Part of why we find it so hard to enjoy the process is because of perfectionism — we find it hard to be comfortable before we have mastered the skill, before we have reached the goal. Perfectionism comes from the belief that it has to be perfect for it to be good. Which leads to the belief that before it is perfect it is bad. This leads to a fear of failure, a fear of trying and a fear of criticism. This is a problem not only because it isn't true and it blocks us from enjoying the process, but also because it actually stunts growth. Learning comes from having insight into what you don't know yet and then learning by reading, observing and then trying it out, failing, adjusting and then trying again and again until you get it right. A fear of failure blocks learning because it stops us from trying.

~

Allow yourself to be a beginner.

~

Enjoying the process is all about relieving yourself of the judgment that gets in the way of enjoying the challenge. It comes from learning to embrace the challenge rather than fear it. It is the judgment of the process that steals the joy. My baby and toddler spend most of their time trying to do things that they cannot do yet and they aren't particularly anxious or frustrated. Why? Because they don't judge the fact that they can't do it yet. They don't mind making mistakes; learning from mistakes is what they do all day long. It is the very mechanism of how they learn. I believe it is that way for all of us when we are young but when we grow up we are taught that making mistakes equals failing. That is when making mistakes goes from being neutral, normal, even an essential part of the learning process, to becoming personal, uncomfortable and an indication of ability. This is where perfectionism is born. In order to learn again, to enjoy the process and the outcome, we need to relearn how to make mistakes and be okay with them, even to expect them.

A recovering perfectionist myself, I now just expect to make mistakes. I want to make mistakes — I even try to celebrate them — because I know that if I am not making mistakes, it means I am not learning. It means I am hiding in my comfort zone just doing the things I know I can do. Everything is hard before it becomes easy. If I am not making mistakes, it means I am not progressing.

Even when my mistakes are really bad and trigger shame and guilt in me, I choose to not get stuck in feeling guilty but instead to be aware, with kindness. Because guilt and shame block learning while kind awareness stimulates learning.

A while ago we had a morning at home in which I became so frustrated that I ended up yelling and storming out the door. Ironically, I was on my way to meet my colleague Shirley to have a meeting about our mindful parenting program. That morning I had been far from the mindful, patient, calm and assertive parent I am learning to be. I was the opposite. On my way there I had a choice: I could go down the guilt and shame path, feel horrible about myself, beat myself up and feel like a fake working on a mindful parenting program, or I could go down the kind awareness path — seeing this mistake as an opportunity for learning, an opportunity for changing something that is not working.

These are tricky moments because part of us wants the guilt. We feel that we deserve it and that it would be unjust to not inflict this punishment on ourselves. We have been so conditioned to believe that mistakes are bad, that we believe *we* are bad when we make mistakes. We think that if we make ourselves feel bad enough we won't do it again. But guilt without awareness of what went wrong, and then changing that in order to avoid making the same mistakes next time, doesn't lead to change. It just leads to self-torture and increased stress levels that will make it even more likely that we will make the same mistake again.

So I chose the second option: to reflect on what happened that morning with kind awareness, asking myself without beating myself up, 'What just happened? What triggered me? What made me react like that? What could I have done differently? What can I do to make sure this doesn't happen again?'

This kind awareness led to insight, which led to learning, which led to practical change that so far has resulted in no more repeats of that situation.

INSIGHT QUESTIONS: PERFECTIONISM

1. What mistakes do you make that leave you feeling guilty or ashamed?

2. Now look with kind awareness at the situations in which that behaviour occurs. Don't beat yourself up but rather analyze the situations without judgment. What happens in them? What triggers you?

3. Why does it make perfect sense that you reacted like that?

4. What can you do to prevent it from happening again? What practical changes can you make to prevent that situation reoccurring?

Trust the process

We have become an outcome-focused generation that has lost sight of the value of the process. As a consequence, we have lost our biggest source of sustainable happiness — the joy that comes from the process not just the outcome. For example:

» We don't study to learn, but to pass the test.

» We don't work because we love it, but to pay our bills.

» We don't cook for the enjoyment of cooking, but to get dinner on the table.

» We visit our friends or family not to enjoy spending time with them, but so we have met the obligation.

» We want the lesson, but not the learning process.

» We want to be strong, but not to be challenged.

» We want great relationships without investing in them.

» We want shortcuts over experience.

Stress and a lack of energy make us more outcomes focused. On days that I am too stressed or don't have enough energy in my system, I often find myself thinking, 'I just have to get through this day, tonight I can relax.' Being present for the process uses up energy and when there is a lack of energy or an overflow of things that need to be done, our brain conserves energy by making us 'not present' with the process and limits our focus to the end goal. That way we can go on energy-conserving autopilot mode during the process and 'wake up' when we have arrived at our destination. In this state, it is easy to fall into the trap of believing that the happiness comes from the outcome. This is true when you are only present with the outcome or 'awake' for the outcome. When you fall into this habit you end up needing more and more outcomes and achievements to feel happy. This usually leads to unsatisfying and fleeting happiness.

Advertising

One industry that knows we have fallen into this trap is the advertising industry. Just think of a few ads. A handsome and successful guy driving a big car on an empty windy road through the fields. A beautiful woman under the shower, washing her hair with her eyes closed and a gentle smile on her face, soaking up the moment. A couple that looks deep into each other's eyes, both with a flirtatious smile on their face, while they elegantly enjoy their drink. Or a woman doing the dishes looking content, happy and enjoying the process, and feeling a sense of pride and achievement as she looks at her sparkling plates and cups.

Scenes like these speak to us because our brain loves every moment of green-brain activity and that is exactly what these ads are showing you. These ads advertise moments of mindfulness, being present, being connected and enjoying the process, not just the end result. Your brain can't help but want it because it is wired to crave those moments. Each moment of mindfully enjoying the process is like a shot of health to each and every part of your system. So when you watch these ads, either consciously or subconsciously, your brain goes, 'Oh, yes please, give me some of that!' But here is the hook: advertisers have hacked the brain's automatic craving for mindfully enjoying the process and have twisted it by saying to you, 'You will have these mindful moments only when you drive our car, use our shampoo, drink our drink and do your dishes with our dishwashing liquid.' And our brain, not prepared for such corrupt manipulation, falls for it.

Advertising works not because it tricks your brain into thinking you will look like the people on the screen, but because it tricks you into believing you will *feel* like the people on the screen. Just imagine that handsome man driving his car stressed and agitated. No matter how handsome he is it won't be appealing. Or imagine the woman under the shower washing her hair in a rush. Same result: no matter how beautiful she is, you don't want to be her or buy the shampoo. At the core, commercials work because you want to feel like the people in them. You too want to be able to enjoy the process.

We have been tricked and the con has worked. We buy the stuff but it doesn't give us the green-brain moments we want because the product itself doesn't actually teach us how to be present with the process. It just gives us another store-bought outcome that fails to deliver. We own more stuff than ever and are more stressed than ever so they can keep convincing us that when we buy their products we will finally feel like their models are pretending to feel. But it is never true.

The good news is that you can have those moments and they are completely free. The happiness comes from being awake, being present, being part of the process as well as the outcome. You can drive your car and look out of the window, take in the surroundings, breathe deeply and smile. You can wash your hair and focus on the warmth of the water, smell the soap, listen to the sounds and completely soak up the moment. You can go on a date, put away your phone, turn off the TV and look each other in the eye while you flirtatiously sip your green tea. And, yes, you can even do the dishes mindfully, feeling the warm water on your hands, watching the light reflected in the bubbles and feeling content when you look at the clean plates.

Enjoyment of the process comes from being mindfully present in the process. If you see the process as just as important as the outcome, in time the process will become just as enjoyable as the outcome, sometimes even more enjoyable.

A couple of months ago we got chickens and they have taught me an important lesson about the value of the process. Before we had chickens I would buy eggs in the supermarket. I would enjoy eating them and then buy more the following week. I can't say I got any pleasure or enjoyment from the process of going to the supermarket and buying the eggs, I only got enjoyment from the end goal — eating the eggs. Now I save our food scraps and my children feed them to the chickens each morning. Then in the afternoon we go and look in the henhouse to see if they have laid any eggs. Every afternoon there is a moment of anticipation as my son opens up the henhouse. When there is an egg he yells, 'Yes, an egg!' When there is no egg he yells, 'No egg yet, Mama.' When he finds an egg he carefully carries it into the house and if it makes it to the kitchen in one piece he says, 'I was being very careful, Mama!' Then we put it away and the next day we eat it.

Having chickens has completely changed my experience of eating eggs. Now that I am part of the process, I get pleasure from the whole process not just from the end part. I get pleasure from the saving of the food scraps to the actual eating of the egg and everything in between. It all gives me joy. Being connected to the process gives joy at both the process and the outcome, and this can be applied to every single aspect of life.

For example, there is no 'misbehaving' when my child 'misbehaves'; it is a normal part of the process and an opportunity for me to teach him that there is a better way to handle the situation. When I feel flat or stressed, it is an opportunity to look at my daily life with awareness and make the changes I need to make. When I have disconnected from my husband, it isn't a failure; it is an opportunity to notice it with kindness and reconnect. A situation gone horribly wrong isn't a failure, it is an opportunity to learn and grow.

~

It's all about the journey and that's how it's supposed to be.

~

No one has ever reached their goals, found a life of purpose and fulfilment, by just waking up one day and knowing exactly what to do and having all the doors opened for them. That is not how life works. It is not how it is supposed to work. It might look like that from the outside and on Instagram accounts but that is never the full story. In every story of success there are mistakes, detours, lessons, disappointments and loss. But when we look at others we tend to put the spotlight on the success and we forget that the success is only part of the story.

Sometimes people look at my life and tell me, 'Wow, you are so lucky! You have the perfect family and a successful business.' But they don't see the countless hours of work I put in behind the scenes. They don't see the moments of despair and frustration when my oldest child just doesn't listen and the youngest refuses to go to sleep. They don't see the self-doubt, lack of support and financial insecurities. All they see are the highlights. When I look at other mothers in the playground having fun with their kids, I need to be careful not to make the same mistake myself by thinking that their children are always angels, that they never lose their patience, and that their house is an oasis of calm and peace and manners. When I look at other successful people in my field, I need to be careful not to fall into the trap of believing their success has come easy and overnight. It is not true and, even more importantly, it isn't what we should want.

Success isn't supposed to be easy. We are not supposed to be catapulted quickly to the top. There are two reasons for this. The first reason is that, although it might be fun, quick success isn't fulfilling or motivating. When we are rewarded or handed outcomes we haven't worked hard for, we don't really enjoy it — at least not for long. Quick and easy success doesn't teach us hard work and perseverance. It changes our experience of the success and takes away many of the positive attributes. It can even make success meaningless.

The second reason we shouldn't want easy success is that it shapes our character in a bad way. Easy success inflates our ego and feeds arrogance, greed and entitlement. If you have ever been around a child who has been given everything they want, you know they are often called a spoiled brat for a reason. It is not the child's fault but rather that praise given without reason and rewards given without effort have a toxic effect on their character.

Life is all about the journey. The journey is the goal. The journey shapes us and makes us into who we are supposed to be. Our character is shaped by the journey and, in the end, it isn't about your success or your possessions; it is about your character.

INGREDIENT 8:

Enjoyment of the outcome

~

Celebrate every tiny victory.

~

When was the last time you celebrated one of your achievements? When was the last time you threw your hands in the air and let out a big fat woo-hoo! I bet you have to think long and hard to remember. Celebrating your victories is not only something you should do because it is fun, you should do it because it is a crucial element for stress-free, sustainable success.

For some reason, we tend to celebrate some victories more easily than others. We all know the images of athletes celebrating their victories with hugs, cheers, joyful dances and champagne, and winning a board game might wake up the dancing queen in you, but when it comes to more serious topics, we often fail to celebrate what we have achieved. I have been more openly excited about winning a game of chess than I was about graduating, recovering from a broken heart or finishing my first book. It seems we have been conditioned to celebrate only certain successes and to be sober about others.

Interestingly enough, there is hardly any scientific research on celebrating successes; even science seems to have overlooked the importance of celebrating victories. Gratitude, on the other hand, has received a lot of attention in the realm of research and I think gratitude and celebrating successes are close cousins, so the research on gratitude should give us some insight into the benefits of celebrating success.

Gratitude

According to research by psychologist Dr Robert Emmons, keeping a gratitude journal results in improved alertness, enthusiasm, determination, optimism and energy. Subjects who kept a daily gratitude journal experienced less depression and stress, were more likely to help others, exercised more consistently and made greater progress toward achieving personal goals. Dr Emmons' research also shows that those who practise an attitude of gratitude tend to be more creative, bounce back more quickly from adversity, have a stronger immune system and have stronger relationships than those who don't practise gratitude. Looking at all the benefits of gratitude, it isn't hard to see how an attitude of gratitude helps with stress-free productivity.

But gratitude and celebrating successes are not the same thing — there is a subtle difference. Gratitude makes me realize my smallness. It makes me reflect on how blessed I am to have what I have and to be able to do what I do. Celebrating successes, on the other hand, makes me realize my greatness. It makes me reflect on how capable I am in certain areas and how my hard work and dedication have paid off in creating improvement and success.

Gratitude is a testimony to what I have been given. Celebrating victories is a testimony to what I have done with what I have been given.

~

Practising gratitude makes you more grateful; celebrating your successes makes you more confident.

~

Just close your eyes and for a moment imagine yourself celebrating a win or a success. You can think back to a moment when you have visibly and excitedly celebrated a victory or you can just imagine yourself winning at something or accomplishing something and then throwing your hands in the air and celebrating. Go ahead, give it a try. The feeling will be even stronger if you do this while standing up and actually putting your hands in the air.

How did that make you feel? Most people would say something along the lines of energized, happy, optimistic or motivated.

Reaching your goal naturally brings happiness and satisfaction but consciously celebrating a success takes it to another level. It is acknowledging to yourself that you have changed, you have grown and you are now able to do something you couldn't do before. Even if it was a small step or a small win, you did it and you are changed because of it. Consciously celebrating this boosts your confidence which, in turn, shifts your perspective. It makes you see yourself as more able and challenges seem less daunting.

There, in the mix of boosted happiness, confidence and positivity, will be a gentle calling to take on the next challenge: a desire to do it again, to aim for the next level, to do something even bigger and better. Celebrating your success is just as much the end point of a cycle of learning and achieving as it is the beginning of a new cycle of learning and achieving.

When we were visiting family and friends in the Netherlands last winter, it snowed. We got an old sledge from the attic and took it to a park. In the park is a hill and we pulled the sledge up it so that we could ride down the hill at full speed. My then three-year-old son was scared and didn't want to go down. After watching us a few times and seeing how much fun we were having, he reluctantly wanted to give it a try. I sat in the front, he sat at the back and as we were going down the hill at high speed, he was yelling, 'Slower Mama, slower!' But there was no way to slow down and when we got to the bottom I yelled out, 'Yes, you did it!' He smiled and said, 'Let's do it again, Mama!' The second time, instead of yelling, 'Slower, slower!' he was shouting, 'Go faster, go faster!'

As soon as we achieve something our confidence instantly grows. We start to think we did it once so we can do it again. As our confidence grows so do our goals. I believe this is a very powerful mechanism. It is the green-brain alternative to the orange-brain cycle of always working toward the next thing on the to-do list without really enjoying what we have. The orange-brain achievement cycle tricks us into believing that the next thing on the to-do list or on the wish list will finally transport us into happiness. The green-brain achievement cycle starts with happiness, turns it into celebration and the acknowledgement of new skills, which leads to confidence, and then naturally bigger, greater goals flow from that.

Why we fail to celebrate

I have been able to identify three reasons why I fail to celebrate and you may recognize these in yourself:

» Discounting many things as too small to celebrate.

» Tall poppy syndrome.

» Rushing into focusing on the next goal.

Discounting many things as too small to celebrate is one reason we fail to celebrate our successes. What was once hard has now become easy and when it is easy we don't see it as celebration material. But why not? Why not celebrate the little things, the little victories? Why don't I celebrate that it's a new day, that I have made it through a three-week visit of my mother-in-law, that I have made it through yet another morning of writing, that I have finally quit Facebook or that I went for a run this morning even though it was only for five minutes?

To cultivate a habit of celebrating we can't just wait around for the big hits, we need to start celebrating the small victories.

What small things can you think of that you can celebrate? Write them down and allow yourself to get excited about them, no matter how small they are. Give yourself permission to be proud of them, no matter how insignificant they may seem. Pat yourself on the back and remind yourself that you did it!

Another reason why some of us (including myself) shun away from celebrating our successes is what I call 'the success complex'. We want to do great things and at the same time there is a strong need in most of us to blend in and not stand out. We are born with a hunger to learn and grow and excel and at the same time we fear that if we do excel we will be judged and rejected by others. This inevitably creates tension and if it doesn't make us hold back when it comes to succeeding, it will make us shy away from celebrating our successes.

I remember as a child being confused by the conflicting messages I received. On the one hand I was told to always do my best, but when I did and excelled at something I noticed it somehow backfired. Other children teased me, and my parents didn't comment on my accomplishments because they somehow thought it would make my siblings feel like they were favouring me. I was painfully aware that others somehow were made uncomfortable by my successes.

In Dutch culture, equality and being humble are two very important values, which unfortunately can lead to tall poppy syndrome. Tall poppy syndrome has been described in many European cultures and also in Australia and New Zealand. It is the tendency to 'cut down' the tall poppies, the successful people who stand out from the crowd, in an effort to make everyone equal again. Not everyone notices tall poppy syndrome because it is often displayed very subtly. But even subtle cultural patterns can influence your thoughts and feelings greatly. If you have grown up in a culture that has tall poppy syndrome, it is understandable that when you succeed at something you don't want to shout it from the rooftops but instead would rather hide. Being a tall poppy means, after all, that you are at risk of having your head chopped off.

Strangely, tall poppy syndrome has influenced me to the point that success and embarrassment have gone hand in hand for a long time. This started to shift when, on a trip to Indonesia, as I was browsing through a gift shop, I saw a quote by Marianne Williamson written on a poster:

~

Our deepest fear is not that we are inadequate. Our deepest fear is that we are powerful beyond measure. It is our light, not our darkness that most frightens us. We ask ourselves, Who am I to be brilliant, gorgeous, talented, and fabulous? Actually, who are you not to be? You are a child of God. Your playing small does not serve the world. There is nothing enlightened about shrinking so that other people will not feel insecure around you. We are all meant to shine, as children do.

~

When I look at my daughter, who learned to walk at nine months, I see a shining child who is proud of and satisfied with the fact that her efforts have paid off and she can now walk. She doesn't look at other babies who at nine months can barely sit up and wonder if her walking might make them feel inadequate. She shines and is excited about her own walking skills; she can't stop showing the whole world what she can do. The other babies don't envy her and they don't resent her for being able to do something they can't. If anything, they will learn to walk sooner because they have 'one of their own' showing them how to do it.

The final reason we don't celebrate our victories is that we are often rushing on to the next goal. People who are very achievement-focused can spend a lot of time focusing on their to-do list (the orange-brain state). In this brain state we can feel uncomfortable with where we are at because it is not where we want to be, and by the time we reach our goal we have a fleeting moment of happiness (a shot of dopamine in the brain), but it doesn't take long until we set our sights on the next goal and begin to feel lacking because we are not at this next goal yet.

For example, I know I will really love our house once we have renovated the bathroom, but when the bathroom is renovated, the old kitchen will really bother me. I'll be so happy and relieved when Project A is finished, but then only after Project B is finished will I really have peace of mind.

When I earn X amount per year we can live comfortably and I won't have to worry about money anymore. However, by the time I earn X amount, I just know that if we can secure Y more per year, I won't have to worry about money anymore.

You keep moving the goalposts and that's fine because you have big dreams and goals, but the problem is that you have tied your happiness and celebration to the moving goalposts that you might never reach because there will always be another goal. You are always looking ahead to the next thing on the to-do list. For people stuck in this cycle, life can feel like a treadmill — they are working so hard but never 'arrive'. They are not enjoying the process and they are not enjoying the wins because there is always another goal right around the corner. The good news is that this can change. You can learn to enjoy the process and you can learn to cultivate the art of celebrating your successes, have lasting enjoyment of them and work towards new goals at the same time.

Create a habit of celebrating

Every success, no matter how small, is worthy of celebration. You don't need balloons, bubbles or a stage to celebrate. Cultivating the art of celebrating successes is something that happens within; it is the attitude of celebration that matters most. And, like anything, this attitude of celebration is a skill that can be trained. You become better and better at it by first of all paying attention to the small successes and letting them be followed by a confident smile. Give yourself a pat on the back or a mental high-five every time you notice a small win.

Celebrating your successes is a valuable skill to have and it will help you achieve even more because you are creating your own rewards and consciously applying them to what you want to do more of. Our brain is wired to seek rewards, to seek that approving smile or nod. You don't need anyone else to give it to you; you can give it to yourself. By doing so you are creating the rewards your brain craves and keeping yourself securely on track with the positive things you are doing, because we are automatically driven to do more of whatever is rewarded. Making the most of your wins by really celebrating them creates new energy and strengthens motivation to create more wins in that area.

So as I wrap up my writing for today, I congratulate myself for making it through yet another morning of writing. I give myself a mental high-five and a 'Well done, you!' I will ignore how awkward this makes me feel and how over the top it sounds to my own ears because I know the power celebration has on the brain. I know it will boost my energy and confidence and that it will help me stick to my goals and finish this book.

The reverse gap

In Chapter 2 I discussed a technique called 'the reverse gap', where you reverse your vision for the future by reflecting on how far you have come from the past. One way to become better at celebrating your successes is to use 'the reverse gap'. Our habit is to look at everything we want and everything we need to get done and notice the gap between where we are now and where we want to be. The reverse gap uses the same principle but reverses it. Look back to where you have come from and then notice the gap between where you used to be and where you are now. Simply notice how far you've come already and celebrate that.

The need to grow is wired into our DNA and achievements are proof of that growth. It is part of being human to want to grow and learn and expand. Learning to celebrate your victories won't make you arrogant; you only become arrogant when you believe there is nothing left to learn. Celebrating your successes will make you more confident and eager to learn even more.

INSIGHT QUESTIONS: THE REVERSE GAP

1. Right now, look at what you have accomplished in the last six months or in the last year and write it down. You can include big wins and small wins. It can include things you have done but also things you have stopped doing. The more specific you make it the better, and remember that it doesn't have to be perfect or exactly as you would like it to be to deserve a place on your achievements list.

   In the last six to twelve months I have:

2. Then with kind awareness look at your list of accomplishments, look at what you have done and what you have achieved. If you notice any discomfort, simply notice it with kindness. Your discomfort makes perfect sense given the culture or the family you come from and your past experiences. Notice it with kindness and then turn your attention back to your list of achievements. What would you say if you were talking to a friend who has worked hard and accomplished the same things? Write it down and say it to yourself.

Conclusion

I hope that by reading this book you now know your brain a little better. I hope the book has given you insights, a-ha moments and new ideas on how to reach your goals faster and enjoy the process more. Most of all, I hope that it has instilled in you the knowledge that you can create a life you are proud of and it can be done without sacrificing your health, your joy or your relationships.

Living from the green brain every day might seem impossible, and sometimes life changes need to be made in order to make your dream a possibility, but all this can be done. Each little step closer to living from that green-brain state and approaching productivity from a mindful perspective is a step away from the unsustainable orange–red-brain productivity loop and a step towards reaching your goals without stressing out.

My recipe for reaching your goals without stressing out is this:

1. Take a green brain

You can recognize the green-brain state by a calm, present mind and kind and non-judgmental thoughts. You can train yourself to spend more and more time in the green brain by finding out what naturally activates it and consciously increasing your daily green-brain triggers and, where possible, reducing your red-brain triggers. Training your thoughts using mindfulness is also a highly effective way to increase your green-brain time and become more in control of your brain state. Activating your green brain is like starting your car and putting it in the right gear. Your green brain provides clarity, sharpness and the energy to get going.

2. Add a few clear goals

Next, you add a goal — something you want to achieve. You can have personal goals, work goals, family goals — anything you want to focus on. Goals can be big or small. The key to setting goals is to make them conscious, clear and specific. Living without goals is like driving without knowing where you want to go. Clear and conscious goals give direction. They prevent you from going around in circles and wasting precious time and energy.

3. Add sustained focus

It is so easy to become distracted. Life gets busy, things go wrong and before you know it, your goals are put on the backburner and you are back doing the same old things you were doing before. In order to stay on track, it helps to create habits that improve your focus. Training your focus helps to avoid detours and prevents you from getting lost. Keeping track of your focus will make you achieve your goals faster.

4. Mix in plenty of energy

Working towards goals often equals creating change, which takes up tremendous amounts of energy, and most of us have hardly any energy to spare. We can optimize our energy levels by understanding what creates energy and optimizing it. By making small changes, we can increase energy production and optimize output so we have more energy left to actually do the things we want.

5. Sprinkle in a hint of passion

The biggest energy booster is passion. Passion unlocks our hidden reservoirs of not only energy but also strength and courage. When we are passionate about something we are almost unstoppable. So either adjusting your goals to ones that activate your passion or finding the passion within your current goals will make you all the more likely to succeed.

6. Stir in perseverance

The journey isn't always fun and real success never comes easy. You will bump into obstacles along the way, it is simply inevitable. So you need perseverance, otherwise you will give up. Learning to keep going when the going gets tough is essential.

7. Then allow it to sit for a while

Once you understand that it is not just about reaching your goal as soon as possible, but to experience the whole journey, you can then remove your harsh judgments from the mistakes you make, turn them into learning opportunities and begin to truly enjoy the process. You don't climb the mountain just for the view. You don't listen to music just to hear the final notes. It is all about the journey. It is the journey that shapes us; arriving at the top — that's the cherry on the cake.

8. Enjoy the sweet taste of success and repeat

Then, when your destination is in sight and you have finally arrived, there is only one thing left to do and that is to celebrate. Be happy and applaud yourself because your hard work has paid off! You should celebrate because it is fun, but there is also a more important reason. Celebration of victories strengthens confidence. This catapults you into more passion-filled, green-brain goal setting and gives you the motivation and energy to continue chasing after your dreams.

Stress-free productivity is not a linear process with a starting point and an end point. It is a cycle.

All the elements work together like the nuts and bolts in an engine. If one of the elements isn't in place or isn't working well, the whole system suffers. However, you don't have to be perfect in any of the elements to experience stress-free productivity. You can start to cultivate it at any time by making small changes here and there.

Finding better ways to achieve your goals matters, not because your achievements define you, but because how you spend your days shapes your character. While you are here on earth you might as well spend your time doing something you enjoy and can truly be proud of.

~

Life is amazing. And then it's awful. And then it's amazing again. And in between the amazing and the awful it's ordinary and mundane and routine. Breathe in the amazing, hold on through the awful, and relax and exhale during the ordinary. That's just living heartbreaking, soul-healing, amazing, awful, ordinary life. And it's breathtakingly beautiful.

— *L R Knost*

~

References

Ingredient 1: The green brain

Kathryn Birnie, Michael Speca and Linda E Carlson, 'Exploring self-compassion and empathy in the context of mindfulness-based stress reduction (MBSR)', *Stress and Health*, December 2010.

Richard J Davidson, Jon Kabat-Zinn, Jessica Schumacher, Melissa Rosenkranz, Daniel Muller, Saki F Santorelli, Ferris Urbanowksi, Anne Harrington, Katherine Bonus and John F Sheridan, 'Alterations in brain and immune function produced by mindfulness meditation', *Psychosomatic Medicine*, July 2003.

Ian Donald, Paul Taylor, Sheena Johnson, Cary Cooper, Susan Cartwright and Susannah Robertson, 'Work environments, stress and productivity: An examination using ASSET', *International Journal of Stress Management*, November 2005.

Jane Raymond and Jennifer L O'Brien, 'Under pressure: The impact of stress on decision making', *Association for Psychological Science*, September 2009.

Amy FT Arnsten, 'Stress signalling pathways that impair prefrontal cortex structure and function', *Nature Reviews Neuroscience*, June 2009.

Franziska Plessow, Rico Fischer, Clemens Kirschbaum and Thomas Goschke, 'Inflexibly focused under stress: Acute psychosocial stress increases shielding of action goals at the expense of reduced cognitive flexibility with increasing time lag to the stressor', *Journal of Cognitive Neuroscience*, November 2011.

Aaron J Gruber, Gwendolyn G Calhoon, Igor Shusterman, Geoffrey Schoenbaum, Matthew R Roesch and Patricio O'Donnell, 'More is less: A disinhibited prefrontal cortex impairs cognitive flexibility', *Journal of Neuroscience*, December 2010.

Esther K Papies, Lawrence W Barsalou and Ruud Custers, 'Mindful attention prevents mindless impulses', *Social Psychological and Personality Science*, May 2012.

Sian L Beilock and Rob Gray, 'From attentional control to attentional spillover: A skill-level investigation of attention, movement, and performance outcomes', *Human Movement Science*, December 2012.

Ingredient 2: Setting clear goals

Barry J Zimmerman, Albert Bandura, Manuel Martinez-Pons, 'Self-motivation for academic attainment: The role of self-efficacy beliefs and personal goal setting', *American Educational Research Journal*, March 2008.

Ingredient 3: Focus

Wendy Wood, Jeffrey M Quinn, Deborah A Kashy, 'Habits in everyday life: Thought, emotion, and action', *Journal of Personality and Social Psychology*, December 2002.

Meryl Reis Louis and Robert I Sutton, 'Switching cognitive gears: From habits of mind to active thinking', *Human Relations*, January 1991.

Mandar S Jog, Yasuo Kubota, Christopher I Connolly, Viveka Hillegaart, Ann M. Graybiel, 'Building neural Representations of Habits', *Science*, November 1999.

Kyle S Smith and Ann M Graybiel, 'A dual operator view of habitual behavior reflecting cortical and striatal dynamics', *Neuron*, June 2013.

Wendy Wood, Leona Tam, Melissa Guerrero Witt, 'Changing circumstances, disrupting habits', *Journal of Personality and Social Psychology*, June 2005.

Roy A Wise, 'Dopamine and food reward: Back to the elements', *American Journal of Physiology, Regulatory, Integrative and Comparative Physiology*, January 2004.

Ingredient 4: Energy

Bas Verplanken, Astrid G Herabadi, Judith A Perry and David H Silvera, 'Consumer style and health: The role of impulsive buying in unhealthy eating', *Psychology and Health*, February 2007.

Laura McMillan, Lauren Owen, Marni Kras, Andrew Scholey, 'Behavioural effects of a 10-day Mediterranean diet. Results from a pilot study evaluating mood and cognitive performance', *Appetite*, February 2011.

Felice N Jacka, Peter J. Kremer, Eva R Leslie, Michael Berk, George C Patton, John W Toumbourou and Joanne W Williams, 'Associations between diet quality and depressed mood in adolescents: Results from the Australian Healthy Neighbourhoods Study', *Australian and New Zealand Journal of Psychiatry*, April 2010.

Adrienne O'Neil, Shae E Quirk, Siobhan Housden, Sharon L Brennan, Lana J. Williams, Julie A Pasco, Michael Berk and Felice N Jacka, 'Relationship between diet and mental health in children and adolescents: A systematic review', *American Journal of Health-System Pharmacy*, September 2014.

LJ Stevens, SS Zentall, JL Deck, ML Abate, BA Watkins, SR Lipp, JR Burgess, 'Essential fatty acid metabolism in boys with attention-deficit hyperactivity disorder', *The American Journal of Clinical Nutrition*, October 1995.

JR Burgess, L Stevens, W. Zhang, L Peck, 'Long-chain polyunsaturated fatty acids in children with attention-deficit hyperactivity disorder', *The American Journal of Clinical Nutrition*, January 2000.

E Konofal, M Lecendreux, I Arnulf, MC Mouren, 'Iron deficiency in children with attention-deficit hyperactivity disorder', *Archives of Pediatrics and Adolescent Medicine*, 2004.

M Bekaroglu, Y Aslan, Y Gedik, O Deger, H Mocan, E Erduran, C Karahan, 'Relationships between serum free fatty acids and zinc, and attention deficit hyperactivity disorder: A research note', *Journal of Child Psychology and Psychiatry*, February 1996.

T Kozielec, B Starobrat-Hermelin, 'Assessment of magnesium levels in children with attention deficit hyperactivity disorder (ADHD)', *Magnesium Research Journal*, June 1997.

P Toren, S Eldar, BA Sela, L Wolmer, R Weitz, D Inbar, S Koren, A Reiss, R Weizman, N Laor, 'Zinc deficiency in attention-deficit hyperactivity disorder', *Biological Psychiatry*, December 1996.

M Bilici, F Yildirim, S Kandil, M Bekaroglu, S Yildirmis, O Deger, M Ulgen, A Yildiran, H Aksu, 'Double-blind, placebo-controlled study of zinc sulfate in the treatment of attention deficit hyperactivity disorder', *Progress in Neuro-Psychopharmacology and Biological Psychiatry*, January 2004.

B Starobrat-Hermelin, T Kozielec, 'The effects of magnesium physiological supplementation on hyperactivity in children with attention deficit hyperactivity disorder (ADHD). Positive response to magnesium oral loading test', *Magnesium Research Journal*, June 1997.

JR Hibbeln, 'Fish consumption and major depression', *Lancet*, April 1998.

S Noaghiul, JR Hibbeln, 'Cross-national comparisons of seafood consumption and rates of bipolar disorders', *American Journal of Psychiatry*, December 2003.

JR Hibbeln, NS Jr, 'Omega-3 fatty acids and psychiatric disorders: Current status of the field in vitamin D: Molecular biology, physiology, and clinical applications', *Human Press*, 1999.

Virginie Rondeau, Hélène Jacqmin-Gadda, Daniel Commenges, Catherine Helmer and Jean-François Dartigues, 'Aluminum and silica in drinking water and the risk of Alzheimer's disease or cognitive decline: Findings from 15-year follow-up of the PAQUID cohort', *American Journal of Epidemiology*, January 2010.

Christopher Exley, Emily R House, 'Aluminium in the human brain', *Chemical Monthly*, November 2010.

RA Yokel, 'The toxicology of aluminum in the brain: A review', *Neurotoxicology*, October 2000.

Ambreen Mirza, Andrew King, Claire Troakes, Christopher Exley, 'Aluminium in brain tissue in familial Alzheimer's disease', *Journal of Trace Elements in Medicine and Biology*, March 2017.

Christina R Tyler and Andrea M Allan, 'The effects of arsenic exposure on neurological and cognitive dysfunction in human and rodent studies: A review', *Current Environment Health Report*, March 2014.

Molly Tolins, Mathuros Ruchirawat, Philip Landrigan, 'The developmental neurotoxicity of arsenic: Cognitive and behavioral consequences of early life exposure', *Annals of Global Health*, August 2014.

Vishal Desai and Stephen G Kaler, 'Role of copper in human neurological disorders', *The American Journal of Clinical Nutrition*, September 2008.

RU Halden, 'Plastics and health risks', *Annual Review of Public Health*, 2010.

MI Wouters, RM van Soesbergen, 'Disease caused by lack of sunlight: Rickets and osteomalacia', *Nederlands tijdschrift voor geneeskunde*, March 1999.

Scott T Weiss, Augusto A Litonjua, 'Maternal diet vs lack of exposure to sunlight as the cause of the epidemic of asthma, allergies and other autoimmune diseases', *Thorax*, September 2007.

Michael F Holick, 'Vitamin D and sunlight: Strategies for cancer prevention and other health benefits', *Clinical Journal of the American Society of Nephrology*, September 2008.

Lulu Xie, Hongyi Kang, Qiwu Xu, Michael J Chen, Yonghong Liao, Meenakshisundaram Thiyagarajan, John O'Donnell, Daniel J Christensen, Charles Nicholson, Jeffrey J Iliff, Takahiro Takano, Rashid Deane, Maiken Nedergaard, 'Sleep drives metabolite clearance from the adult brain', *Science*, October 2013.

Ilene Rosen, Phyllis Gimotty, Judy Shea, Lisa Bellini, 'Evolution of sleep quantity, sleep deprivation, mood disturbances, empathy, and burnout among interns', *Academic Medicine*, January 2006.

Yavuz Selvi, Mustafa Gulec, Mehmet Yucel Agargun, Lutfullah Besiroglu, 'Mood changes after sleep deprivation in morningness–eveningness chronotypes in healthy individuals', *Journal of Sleep Research*, August 2007.

Daniel J Taylor, Kenneth L Lichstein, H Heith Durrence, Brant W Reidel, Andrew J Bush, 'Epidemiology of insomnia, depression, and anxiety', *Sleep*, November 2005.

SA Paluska and TL Schwenk, 'Physical activity and mental health', *Sports Medicine*, March 2000.

Paula N Stein, Robert W Motta, 'Effects of aerobic and nonaerobic exercise on depression and self-concept', *Perceptual and Motor Skills*, February 1992.

Robert E Thayer, *Calm Energy: How people regulate mood with food and exercise*, Oxford University Press, 2001.

Ichiro Kawachi, Lisa F Berkman, 'Social ties and mental health', *Journal of Urban Health*, September 2001.

William W Dressler, 'Extended family relationships, social support, and mental health in a southern black community', *Journal of Health and Social Behavior*, March 1985.

James S House, Karl R Landis, Debra Umberson, 'Social relationships and health', *Science*, July 1988.

Gwenn Schurgin O'Keeffe, Kathleen Clarke-Pearson, 'The impact of social media on children, adolescents, and families', *Pediatrics*, April 2011.

Liu yi Lin, Jaime E Sidani, Ariel Shensa, Ana Radovic, Elizabeth Miller, Jason B Colditz, Beth L Hoffman, Brian A Primack, 'Association between social media use and depression among U.S. young adults', *Depression and Anxiety*, January 2016.

Kimberly S Young and Robert C Rogers, 'The relationship between depression and internet addiction', *Cyberpsychology and Behavior*, January 2009.

Dan Ariely and Dan Zakay, 'A timely account of the role of duration in decision making', *Acta Psychologica*, August 2001.

Shai Danziger, Jonathan Levav, Liora Avnaim-Pesso, 'Extraneous factors in judicial decisions', *Proceedings of the National Academy of Sciences*, February 2011.

D Dragone, 'I am getting tired: Effort and fatigue in intertemporal decision-making', *Journal of Economic Psychology*, 2009.

A John Maule, G Robert Hockey, L Bdzola, 'Effects of time-pressure on decision-making under uncertainty: Changes in affective state and information processing strategy', *Acta Psychologica*, June 2000.

Ingredient 5: Passion

Abiola Keller, Kirstin Litzelman, Lauren E Wisk, Torsheika Maddox, Erika Rose Cheng, Paul D Cresswell and Whitney P Witt, 'Does the perception that stress affects health matter? The association with health and mortality', *Health Psychology*, September 2012.

JP Jamieson, MK Nock and WB Mendes, 'Mind over matter: Reappraising arousal improves cardiovascular and cognitive responses to stress', *Journal of Experimental Psychology General*, August 2012.

Ingredient 6: Perseverance

Carol S Dweck, 'The secret to raising smart kids', *Scientific American*, January 2015.

Tarmo Strenze, 'Intelligence and socioeconomic success: A meta-analytic review of longitudinal research', *Intelligence*, October 2007.

Tom Farsides, Ruth Woodfield, 'Individual differences and undergraduate academic success: The roles of personality, intelligence, and application', *Personality and Individual Differences*, May 2003.

L Blackwell, K Trzesniewski and CS Dweck, 'Implicit theories of intelligence predict achievement across an adolescent transition: A longitudinal study and an intervention', *Child Development*, February 2007.

Chia-Jung Tsay, Mahzarin R Banaji, 'Naturals and strivers: Preferences and beliefs about sources of achievement', *Journal of Experimental Social Psychology*, March 2011.

Angela L Duckworth, Christopher Peterson, Michael D Matthews, Dennis R Kelly, 'Grit: Perseverance and passion for long-term goals.' *Journal of Personality and Social Psychology*, June 2007.

Angela L Duckworth, Lauren Eskreis-Winkler, 'True grit', *The Observer*, April 2013.

David Scott Yeager and Carol S Dweck, 'Mindsets that promote resilience: When students believe that personal characteristics can be developed', *Educational Psychologist*, October 2012.

CS Dweck, 'Even geniuses work hard', *Educational Leadership*, September 2010.

Ingredient 7: Enjoyment of the process

Margaret M Clifford, 'Students need challenge, not easy success', *Educational Leadership*, September 1990.

Ingredient 8: Enjoyment of the outcome

Alex M Wood, Jeffrey J Froh, Adam WA Geraght, 'Gratitude and well-being: A review and theoretical integration', *Clinical Psychology Review*, November 2010.

Philip C Watkins, Kathrane Woodward, Tamara Stone, Russell L Kolts, 'Gratitude and happiness: Development of a measure of gratitude, and relationships with subjective well-being', *Social Behavior and Personality: An International Journal*, 2003.

Acknowledgments

This book has been influenced by many people including my teachers, mentors, supervisors, clients, family and colleagues, but also various writers, researchers and experts. Thank you all for sharing your knowledge and for influencing and inspiring many others, including me. The work of the following professors, psychologists and counsellors have greatly contributed to important parts of this book:

~

Jan Bernard

Pauline Skeates

Ann Graybiel

Angela Duckworth

Carol Dweck

~

Index